WORDS FROM THE WISE

KNOWING AND ENJOYING GOD

TIM CHALLIES

GRAPHICS BY JULES KOBLUN

HARVEST HOUSE PUBLISHERS
EUGENE, OREGON

Cover and interior design by Studio Gearbox
Cover photo © Vitali Bashkatov / Shutterstock

Published in association with Wolgemuth & Associates, Inc.

M is a federally registered trademark of the Hawkins Children's LLC. Harvest House Publishers, Inc., is the exclusive licensee of the trademark.

Knowing and Enjoying God
Text copyright © 2021 by Tim Challies
Artwork copyright © 2021 by Jules Koblun
Published by Harvest House Publishers
Eugene, Oregon 97408
www.harvesthousepublishers.com

ISBN 978-0-7369-8385-3 (hardcover)
ISBN 978-0-7369-8386-0 (eBook)

Library of Congress Cataloging-in-Publication Control Number: 2020055179

Printed in China

21 22 23 24 25 26 27 28 29 / RDS / 10 9 8 7 6 5 4 3 2 1

CONTENTS

INTRODUCTION

It seems fitting to begin this book of quotes with a quote. "Books don't change people, paragraphs do—sometimes sentences."[1] I have always considered reading a book worth the effort if, at the end, it has provided just a few sentences that will remain with me for the long haul. A single paragraph or even a single sentence can change a life.

Many years ago I began to collect quotes as I encountered them in the books I was reading. Eventually I had the idea that I should combine these quotes with graphics to make them more substantial and more shareable. Jules Koblun put her graphic design skills to work to format the text and lay it atop a suitable and beautiful image. These quote graphics, which we call "SquareQuotes," have been shared countless millions of times on social media as if to prove that a single sentence really can make a great difference.[2]

This little book is a collection of SquareQuotes—inspirational quotes accompanied by a devotional. It is structured around the theme of the Christian's relationship with God. Some might refer to this theme as "the spiritual disciplines," but we prefer to speak of "the means of grace." God gives us the great privilege of having a real, living relationship with him, and this relationship is carried out through *means*. The means of grace are the habits we engage in through which we speak to God and he speaks to us, through which we listen to God and he listens to us. They are the habits through which we engage with his body, the church. They are how we enjoy and cultivate the relationship we share with our great God.

The great majority of this book falls into chapters 3, 4, and 5: "We Listen," "We Speak," and "We Belong." These headings refer to our habits of reading the Bible, of praying, and of participating in the local church. But before we can get to those three great habits, we need to lay a foundation. We need to understand the privilege it is to be invited to relate to God in the first place, and the obligation this gives us to form habits through which we can take full advantage of God's gracious invitation to know him and be known by him. Thus we will first explore a few quotes related to the relational nature of God and the importance of spiritual habits.

It is our hope that you will come to enjoy these quotes as much as we have, that you will benefit from these short sentences and the brief devotional writings that accompany them. May these sentences change you as they have changed us and so many others.

GOD
SPEAKS

History began with words. God said, "Let there be light" and with those words began to bring created order from primordial chaos. Through six days of creative labor, God created the heavens and the earth, the seas and the land, the plants and the animals, and then finally, human beings. God brought into existence a man and a woman who were created in his image and after his likeness. These beings were unique in that they were able to speak back, to have a real and living relationship with God.

The great tragedy of this relationship is that these human beings rebelled against their Creator. Already uniquely and lovingly formed in the image of God, they wanted the power and prerogatives of God; they wanted to be their own gods. So they turned on their Creator, making him an enemy, and in so doing they broke the friendship, they broke the relationship.

That could have been the end of humanity or the end of the relationship between God and man. But thanks to God, it was not. How? Why? Read on to find out…

WHAT WERE WE MADE FOR?

TO KNOW GOD.

WHAT AIM SHOULD WE HAVE IN LIFE?

TO KNOW GOD.

WHAT IS THE ETERNAL LIFE THAT JESUS GIVES?

TO KNOW GOD.

WHAT IS THE BEST THING IN LIFE?

TO KNOW GOD.

WHAT IN HUMANS GIVES GOD MOST PLEASURE?

KNOWLEDGE OF
HIMSELF.

—— J.I. PACKER ——

As we consider the spiritual disciplines, or means of grace, it is crucial that we remember not only the great purpose of these habits but also the great blessing they represent. We were made to know God and to be known by God. We were made in the image of God to have a real and living relationship with God. We were the ones who interrupted this relationship through our sin and rebellion, who declared God an enemy rather than a friend. What a blessing, then, that even though we rebelled against God through our sin, he made the way for the relationship to be restored. What an honor that he still invites us to join into that relationship, that friendship. The practices that are the subjects of these devotional writings are the keys to knowing God. It is through the Bible that we learn about the nature of God and the acts of God; it is through prayer that we speak to God and share our hearts with him; it is through fellowship that we join into his body, serve his people, and demonstrate his love. It is because Christianity is intrinsically relational that Packer can say, "What is the best thing in life? To know God." May we never lose the wonder of that great privilege.

When you
come to knowing God,
the initiative lies on His side.
If He does not show Himself,
nothing you can do will
enable you to find Him.

C.S. LEWIS

There are no truly innocent human beings. Each of us has willfully rebelled against God, but even if we hadn't, we would still be tainted by the sin of Adam, for "by the one man's disobedience the many were made sinners" (Romans 5:19). In Paul's great letter to the church in Rome, he explains that in our sinful state, we actively suppress any knowledge of God, even denying the undeniable reality of his power and presence in creation. Our thinking about God and the state of our own souls becomes futile, our hearts become darkened, and we behave like fools—for "the fool says in his heart, 'There is no God'" (Psalm 14:1). Yet this is a book about having a genuine relationship with God. How can that be? It is possible only because God has taken the initiative. When we could not and would not reach out to him, he has reached out to us. "For while we were still weak, at the right time Christ died for the ungodly.... God shows his love for us in that while we were still sinners, Christ died for us" (Romans 5:6,8). That's the kind of God we serve—the God who reaches out!

GOD TAKES US
INTO HIS CONFIDENCE AND
SHARES HIS SECRETS WITH US;
GOD FINDS US IGNORANT
AND GIVES US KNOWLEDGE.

———————————

THAT IS WHAT REVELATION MEANS.

J.I. Packer

God takes the initiative in establishing relationship by reaching out to helpless humanity. He reveals himself to the creatures he has made. But what does it mean for him to provide such revelation of himself? John Calvin began his *Institutes* by saying, "Nearly all the wisdom which we possess, that is to say, true and sound wisdom, consists of two parts: the knowledge of God and of ourselves."[3] This is exactly the knowledge God provides us. He takes us into his confidence to share what would otherwise remain hidden from our understanding. He enlightens our minds to know and our hearts to receive the truth about himself and the truth about ourselves, for these are the keys to any true wisdom. God provides such revelation not because we deserve it or are in any way owed it, but only because he is gracious, because he delights to give us those things we do not deserve. Because of his grace, we have access to information that would otherwise remain hidden, information we need if we are to be saved from our sin. Praise God for revealing himself to us!

Revelation is the free act of God
by which He graciously condescends

TO DISPLAY AND REVEAL HIS CHARACTER,

NATURE, AND WILL TO MANKIND.

Erwin Lutzer

God has graciously chosen to initiate relationship with human beings who, left to themselves, deny his power and even his very existence. He does this through revelation—through revealing himself to us. But what is it that he reveals about himself? As Lutzer explains, it is his character, his nature, and his will. I've heard it said that character is who you are when no one is looking. God reveals himself as someone who existed long before there was anyone looking, and then as now, his *character* was marked by love. He has always existed in a loving relationship of Father, Son, and Holy Spirit. We might say his *nature* is his attributes, or the qualities of his "godness." And his *will* includes his desires for humanity. As the one who created us, he is the one who has the right to tell us how we ought to live. How does God reveal all of this? Through what we call general revelation and special revelation. General revelation is what God reveals to all of humanity through what has been made and can be observed by all. Special revelation is what God reveals through special means—most notably through Scripture and its revelation of Jesus Christ.

WHAT ARE THE HEAVENS, THE EARTH,
THE SEA, BUT A SHEET OF ROYAL PAPER,
WRITTEN ALL OVER WITH THE WISDOM
AND POWER OF GOD?

THOMAS BROOKS

Thomas Brooks pictures God's creation as a great sheet of the highest-quality paper that has been set apart for the most noble purpose. This royal paper, paper that's fit for a king and written on by a king, describes the wisdom and power of the one who is over all kings. In Brooks's metaphor, this paper does not contain words, but works—the creative works of a powerful God. On the paper are the innumerable stars, each one made by God, each one known by God, each one named by God (Psalm 147:4). On the paper is the earth itself with its countless plants and animals, its majestic mountains and deep valleys, its tall trees and bright flowers, each of which God declared good and very good (Genesis 1:10,31). On the same paper are the mighty oceans and still seas, the running rivers and great lakes, the many waters teeming with life. Together, the heavens, the earth, and the seas are like words on paper that tell of the surpassing wisdom and inexhaustible strength of a mighty God.

EACH OF US IS UNDER A DIVINE
MANDATE TO BECOME AN AMATEUR
ASTRONOMER, TO PEER INTO THE
INCALCULABLE DEPTHS OF SKY
& SPACE TO BEHOLD THE HANDIWORK
OF OUR OMNIPOTENT CREATOR.

Sam Storms

The great poet David looks to the night skies and pours out his heart in praise to God: "The heavens declare the glory of God, and the sky above proclaims his handiwork. Day to day pours out speech, and night to night reveals knowledge" (Psalm 19:1-2). Notice all the ways that creation is communicating: The heavens are *declaring*, the sky is *proclaiming*, the day is *speaking*, the night is *revealing*. And then notice the content of this communication: The heavens are declaring God's glory, the skies are proclaiming the fact that he has created them, the day and night are revealing the knowledge of his existence. This is exactly why Sam Storms can say that each human being is under a mandate to become an amateur astronomer, to look to the heavens, to see what God has created, and to learn the lessons he means for us to learn. And just as we must look up to the skies, we must also look down to the microscopic world, out to all the plants and animals, and even inward to the human body and soul. In all of it, we see God's handiwork. We see that God is communicating that he exists and that he is powerful.

TO PUT IT IN SIMPLE TERMS,

GENERAL REVELATION PROVIDES ENOUGH KNOWLEDGE
OF GOD TO GET REBELLIOUS PEOPLE LIKE YOU AND ME
INTO TROUBLE, BUT NOT ENOUGH TO GET US OUT OF IT.

WE NEED SOMETHING MORE.

Daryl Wingerd

God has created a beautiful world that is full of wonders, and these wonders serve a purpose—they are meant to evoke awe, which in turn is meant to provoke worship. This was the experience of King David, who said, "When I look at your heavens, the work of your fingers, the moon and the stars, which you have set in place, what is man that you are mindful of him, and the son of man that you care for him?" (Psalm 8:3-4). It is difficult to think great thoughts of ourselves as we gaze into a starlit night sky or stand before the Matterhorn. In this way David studied God's creation, marveled at what he saw, and was stirred to worship. Yet for all the beauty of creation and all it communicates to us, God has deliberately limited its message. Through creation God has revealed "his invisible attributes, namely, his eternal power and divine nature" (Romans 1:20). But through creation God has *not* revealed his plan of salvation. He has not revealed how sinful man can be reconciled to a holy God. For that, there must be another kind of revelation.

WHILE GENERAL REVELATION IS INDEED IMPORTANT, IT IS NOT SUFFICIENT IN ITSELF. IT IS THROUGH SCRIPTURE, NOT NATURE ALONE, THAT WE COME TO KNOW AND ARTICULATE THE PARTICULARS OF THE GOSPEL MESSAGE AND ARE CALLED TO UNIQUELY RESPOND TO IT.

SAM STEPHENS

General revelation serves exactly the purpose God intended for it—it reveals his power and divine nature. But as Sam Stephens points out, its message, though important, is insufficient. Though it tells us about the existence of God, it does not tell us about how to be reconciled to God. To know the message of the gospel, the good news of salvation for sinners, we must have more. Thankfully, God has provided not only general revelation but also special and specific revelation in the Bible. It is in the Bible that we learn more about God and more about ourselves. It is in the Bible that we learn how God has intervened in this world to save us from our rebellion. Ultimately, the Bible is the revelation of Jesus Christ as the Savior of humanity and the King of the world. Where nature is insufficient, the Bible is sufficient—it tells us everything we must know if we are to respond to God in repentance and faith.

For the living God to be known,
He must make Himself known,
and He has done this in the
—— *acts and words* ——
recorded in Scripture.

DONALD BLOESCH

Part of the joy of reading biography is having the opportunity to learn about a person who lived before us. An exceptional biography makes us feel as if we have actually come to know its subject, so that we rejoice in that person's triumphs, grieve over his failures, and weep at his death. There is a sense in which the Bible is a biography, in which it is the story of God. It reveals God by describing what he has done and what he has said, for if the living God is to be known, "He must make Himself known, and He has done this in the acts and words recorded in Scripture." The Bible begins with God speaking: "Let there be light." And the Bible ends with God speaking: "He who testifies to these things says, 'Surely I am coming soon'" (Revelation 22:20). Between those two declarations are 66 books; 1,189 chapters; and just over 31,000 verses, each of which exists to tell us who our God is and what our God has done. If we are to know God, he must make himself known. Through Scripture he has done exactly that.

GOD'S WORD DOES NOT

MERELY IMPART INFORMATION;

IT ACTUALLY CREATES LIFE.

IT'S NOT ONLY DESCRIPTIVE;

IT'S EFFECTIVE TOO.

GOD SPEAKING

IS GOD ACTING.

Michael Horton

The Bible may be a book, but it is a book unlike any other. The Bible is inspired—breathed out by God—and in that way perfectly reflects the mind and will of God. The Bible is also complete, sufficient, inerrant, and infallible. Because the Bible is all these things and so many more, it is powerful and effective. Because it is *God's* Word, it comes with all the power and authority of God—power and authority sufficient to change us from the outside in. As we read the Bible, the Bible reads us. As we study the Bible, the Bible studies us. As we examine its every word, it examines our every thought, our every action, our every desire, our every inclination. It identifies our shortcomings; it calls us to change. But more than that, it provokes and promotes and *causes* that change. How do we know? Because "the word of God is living and active, sharper than any two-edged sword, piercing to the division of soul and of spirit, of joints and of marrow, and discerning the thoughts and intentions of the heart" (Hebrews 4:12). As God speaks through the Bible, God acts through the Bible, for "God speaking *is* God acting."

The God who created us, the God who witnessed our rebellion against him, the God who could have cast us out forever, has graciously invited us to enjoy a restored relationship—a relationship in which we speak to him, we listen as he speaks to us, and we belong to his body and participate in all its benefits. He offers us means of grace—habits through which we relate to him, come to truly know him, and enjoy the benefits associated with him.

Before we look at each of these means of grace, we need to understand the importance of habits, the importance of being disciplined in our relationship with God. For just like any other relationship, this one depends upon time, effort, vulnerability, speaking, listening, and simply enjoying one another. Habits ensure we take full advantage of all God offers us through Christ Jesus.

ADVANCE IN THE CHRISTIAN LIFE COMES
NOT BY THE WORK OF THE HOLY SPIRIT ALONE,
NOR BY OUR WORK ALONE,
BUT BY OUR RESPONDING TO AND
COOPERATING WITH THE GRACE THE
HOLY SPIRIT INITIATES AND SUSTAINS.

Donald Whitney

There are two related truths we need to understand and keep constantly in mind when it comes to our growth as Christians: Advance in the Christian life, which is to say advance in our relationship with God and advance in being like God, comes by a combination of God's work *and* our work. Where justification is a work of God alone, sanctification is a work in which we cooperate. God, by his Spirit, initiates and sustains that work, but we are called to respond to it and cooperate with it. Any relationship depends upon each person pursuing the other, and what's true of our friendships with other human beings is equally true of our friendship with this Divine Being. While God genuinely pursues us, we must also pursue him. Even as he begins the relationship, we must foster it. Even as he reaches out toward us, we must reach toward him. Have you reached out to God today through prayer? Have you listened to his voice through the Scriptures? What are you doing to foster this relationship?

It is the grace of
God that gives us His

"means of grace"

for our ongoing perseverance
and growth and joy this side of the
coming new creation.

DAVID MATHIS

God initiates his grace in our lives by his Holy Spirit and invites us to cooperate with it as we grow in our relationship with him. But what is that grace meant to accomplish in our lives? And how do we sustain a relationship with a Being we cannot see and with whom we cannot converse face to face? God gives us what Christians have long referred to as "means of grace." As we take hold of these means, we grow in knowledge and faith, we persevere in the Christian life, and we experience joy as we await the coming new creation. These means of grace are the disciplines or habits through which we can relate to God in ever-deeper ways. By giving us these means, God shows that we really do have the privilege of relating to him, but he also shows that we cannot relate to him in whatever ways we may want or we may deem suitable. While we can genuinely be friends with God, he is the one who sets the terms and conditions of that friendship. To us falls the joyful privilege of cooperating with his grace according to his means.

ONE MEASURE OF THE GREATNESS OF A MAN IS NOT ONLY THAT HE PRACTICES WHAT HE PREACHES, BUT ALSO THAT HE DOESN'T CONSIDER HIMSELF ABOVE THE ORDINARY MEANS OF GRACE THAT ALL CHRISTIANS NEED.

John Piper

While all of us ought to see evidence of marked growth in our knowledge of God, our relationship with him, and our obedience to him, none of us ever evolves beyond our need for these ordinary means of grace. We never "level up" to such a degree that we gain access to some hidden extraordinary means of grace. We begin the Christian life by building habits that will foster our relationship with God, and these very disciplines are meant to sustain us to the end. In this quote, John Piper talks about the measure of the greatness of a man (or woman), and we know from the Bible that true greatness is marked by humility, for "whoever exalts himself will be humbled, and whoever humbles himself will be exalted" (Matthew 23:12). The humble Christian receives these means of grace as undeserved kindness from God for his growth and joy and perseverance. He never allows himself to think he has so mastered them or so mastered the Christian faith that he is no longer fully and utterly dependent upon such simple, wonderful, ordinary means. As John Newton wrote, "'Tis grace hath brought me safe thus far, and grace will lead me home."

Complacency is a deadly foe of all spiritual growth.

A.W. Tozer

As we live out the Christian life and cooperate with the Holy Spirit through the precious means of grace, we face a number of foes, a number of enemies that mean to derail us from our pursuit of God. Of all those enemies, none may be more prevalent and none more deadly than complacency. If it is humility that keeps us from thinking we have somehow risen above those ordinary means, complacency is that all-too-familiar satisfaction with our own accomplishments. It is that feeling, that conviction even, that we have done enough, that we have done more than enough, that we can now relax our pursuit of God. Yet what God said to Isaiah, he says to us: "This is the one to whom I will look: he who is humble and contrite in spirit and trembles at my word" (Isaiah 66:2). Humility calls us to assess ourselves rightly as remaining so needy and so incomplete, while contrition calls us to be remorseful for how little we truly know of God and how full of sin we still are. Together they call us to commit ourselves to God and to his Word, to tremble before him and to forever desire him.

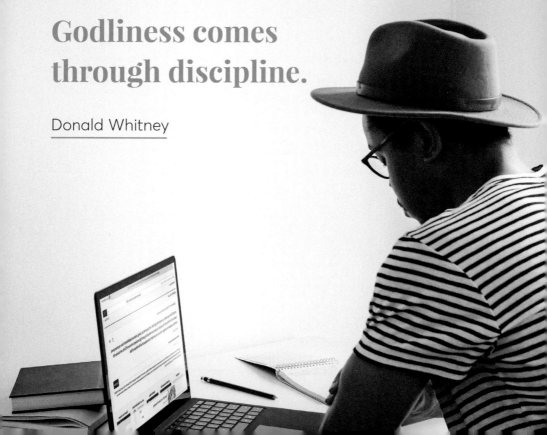

In my own pastoral and personal Christian experience, I can say that I've never known a man or woman who came to spiritual maturity except through discipline.

Godliness comes through discipline.

Donald Whitney

You can't read the New Testament and fail to understand that the Christian life was never meant to be a life of ease. Each of us will encounter adversity and adversaries, and each of us will have to wage war against our fearsome foes—the world, the flesh, and the devil. Then, each of us will also have to labor to come to know God and to grow in our likeness to God. For all these reasons, the Christian life demands a disciplined approach. The apostle Paul often compared Christians to athletes who must train diligently to have any hope of victory. "Every athlete exercises self-control in all things," he said. "They do it to receive a perishable wreath, but we an imperishable. So I do not run aimlessly; I do not box as one beating the air. But I discipline my body and keep it under control" (1 Corinthians 9:25-27). The only way to win the match or to be victorious in the race is to discipline your whole life toward that podium, toward that gold medal. Similarly, the only way to prevail in the Christian life is to discipline your entire existence toward Christlikeness.

*Many, I fear, would like **glory**,*
*who have no wish for **grace**.*

They would fain have
*the wages, **but not the work**;*
*the harvest, **but not the labor**;*
*the reaping, **but not the sowing**;*
*the reward, **but not the battle**.*

J.C. RYLE

Just as Olympic athletes cannot realistically expect to win a gold medal unless they strictly discipline themselves toward victory, Christians cannot hope to prevail in the Christian life unless they take a serious, disciplined approach to it. Yet lurking in the background is always the temptation to hope that we can have the result of diligent labor without the labor itself, that we can have the glorious end we desire without the difficult means. The apostle Paul spoke longingly of "the crown of righteousness" that was awaiting him and all who persevere to the end (2 Timothy 4:8). James told of "the crown of life" that God promised to those who love him and who remain steadfast through trials (James 1:12). J.C. Ryle knew of these crowns and feared that many Christians wanted the glorious reward but without diligence in the means of grace. He feared that many wanted a payday without work, a plentiful harvest without hard labor, a victory parade without a battle. Yet in the Christian life, as in every other area, the rewards are not dispensed indiscriminately, but are recognitions of effort, of diligence, of achievement.

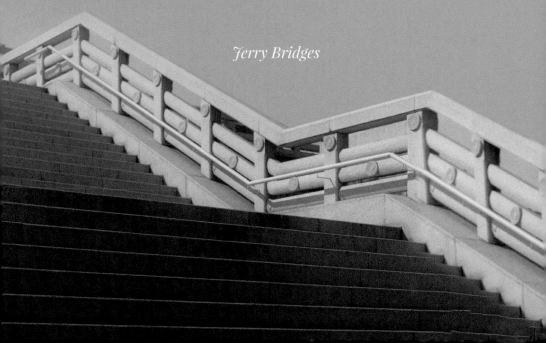

We must remember that the methods of spiritual disciplines are a *means to the end, not the end* themselves.

Jerry Bridges

There is a crucial distinction between means and ends. Ends are the goals we have set our hearts on, while means represent the habits or disciplines through which we can realistically hope to attain those goals. The end of exercise is fitness, and the means is training in both cardio and strength. The great goal of the Christian life is to know God, and the means are the spiritual disciplines. We need to be careful that we maintain this distinction, for as Jerry Bridges warns us, we are prone to make the means of grace an end unto themselves. Instead of understanding the means of grace as the habits through which we come to achieve that great goal of deepening our relationship to God, we can come to see the means of grace as the sum and substance of the Christian life. Instead of pursuing God, we pursue the means, assessing our faith not by our likeness to God, but by the quality or consistency of our reading, prayer, and fellowship. We must always look beyond the means to that great and wonderful and motivating goal of knowing our God.

The final joy in any truly Christian discipline or practice or rhythm of life is, in the words of the apostle,

"THE SURPASSING WORTH OF KNOWING CHRIST JESUS MY LORD"

(Philippians 3:8).

DAVID MATHIS

When it comes to spiritual disciplines, we are apt to confuse the means and the ends. We can so easily slip into believing that good habits of reading the Bible, praying, and fellowshipping with other Christians is the sum and substance of the Christian faith. We can take joy and comfort in the strength of our habits. But like the apostle Paul, we must have a much more noble desire than that, and we must labor toward a much greater joy. As David Mathis says, "The final joy in any truly Christian discipline or practice or rhythm of life is, in the words of the apostle, 'the surpassing worth of knowing Christ Jesus my Lord'" (Philippians 3:8). Knowing Christ Jesus—this is the great goal and the great joy. We read the Bible because it reveals Jesus Christ as divine Savior of the world. We pray so we can have a true and living relationship with God through Christ Jesus. We commit ourselves to fellowship so we can join together with Christ's body, which is the local church. Though the habits may bring joy as we apply ourselves to them, the greater joy comes in the real and living relationship we have as we come to know Jesus Christ.

BEWARE OF IDLENESS.

SATAN SOWS MOST OF HIS SEED IN FALLOW GROUND.

THOMAS WATSON

Watson's warning about idleness is relevant to any area of life, and most Christians quickly come to observe the intimate relationship between idleness and temptation. Charles Spurgeon, who was devoted to the writings of Watson, echoed his mentor when he said, "The most likely man to go to hell is the man who has nothing to do on earth. Idle people tempt the devil to tempt them."[4] While Watson's warning is broad enough to apply to all of life, it is also narrow enough to apply to the Christian's relationship with God. Ground that is fallow has been left idle for a season and is producing no good crops. Lives that are fallow have been left to "go to seed," and Satan will gladly sneak in to sow them with sin. Fallow lives reflect no great devotion to God and no great pursuit of God, but are instead devoted to ease or the pursuit of endless entertainment. Watson warns that as we ease off in pursuing our relationship with God, we open ourselves to the temptations of the devil, for a fallow field bears weeds rather than wheat, and a fallow life bears sin rather than sanctification.

Your worst days are never so bad that you are beyond the reach of God's grace.

And your best days are never so good that you are beyond the need of God's grace.

There can be a subtle danger inherent in a long focus on the spiritual disciplines and the building of good habits. If we are not careful, we can begin to take a kind of comfort in our habits that makes us think *they* are what makes us acceptable to God. Even though we know we have been saved by grace through faith, we can still believe that God's ongoing favor toward us depends upon the strength of our devotional lives. Conversely, when our habits are disrupted or neglected, we can feel a kind of fear that our poor habits have made us unacceptable to God. And this is where we need this reminder from Jerry Bridges that even on our worst and most neglectful days, God does not suddenly begin to relate to us by works rather than grace. God's love for us does not waver on the days we neglect Scripture and prayer. But we also need to be reminded that our best actions on our best days are never so good that they make us more acceptable to God or more righteous before him. Through the gospel we have been accepted once and for all, not on the basis of who we are, but on the basis of Christ's sacrifice!

We must never stop marveling at this wonderful truth: God speaks. And since God speaks, we can listen. We *must* listen, for the fact that God speaks puts a moral obligation on us to listen to what he says. We are responsible to listen so we can know, and we are responsible to know so we can obey.

As we have seen, God speaks through what he has made, and God speaks through the Bible. And while God's voice in creation is powerful, it is also deliberately limited. It speaks of his ability and his power and his wrath, but it does not speak of his plan to redeem humanity. It is through the Scriptures that God speaks most clearly, most powerfully, and most effectually. The Scriptures are a means of grace through which we grow in our relationship with him, through which we experience in deeper and more profound ways the benefits of our redemption, in which we learn about his plan to save the world through the birth, life, death, and resurrection of his Son, Jesus Christ. In this section we will learn about what the Bible is, what the Bible does, why we have such desperate need for it, and why we must build the habits of reading it, pondering it, and applying it.

The Bible is an

armory of heavenly weapons,

a laboratory of infallible medicines,

a mine of exhaustless wealth.

It is a guidebook for every road,

a chart for every sea,

a medicine for every malady,

and a balm for every wound.

Thomas Guthrie

Every true Christian can attest to the unique value of the Bible. Some do this by describing the attributes of the Bible, and they use doctrinal words like "inspiration," "canonicity," "inerrancy," "infallibility," and "sufficiency." Each of these is useful in describing something that is true about God's Word. But there is another way to describe the Bible, and that is to describe the effects it has on the Christian mind, heart, and life. That is the tactic Thomas Guthrie employs in these words. As he waxes eloquent, he tells what has proven true about the Bible as he has committed himself to reading it, meditating upon it, and living it out. It has proven its value as weaponry in the battle against spiritual foes, as a laboratory researching cures for spiritual maladies, and as a rich source of treasure in the accumulating of wisdom. It has proven itself a guide to the pathways of life and a chart to navigate the stormy seas of trial and tribulation. It has been to him medicine that brings healing to every spiritual illness, and it has been a soothing ointment for every one of life's deep wounds. The Bible proves all of this to those who commit themselves to it.

The Bible is alive;
it speaks to me.
It has feet;
it runs after me.
It has hands;
it lays hold of me!

Martin Luther

I wonder if you noticed that in this quote, Martin Luther employs the literary technique of anthropomorphism—he applies the attributes of a person to the Bible. He declares that the Bible has qualities of life: that it has a voice and can speak, that it has feet and can run, that it has hands and can grasp. If you have studied the life of Luther, you'll know that in a time of great spiritual torment he committed himself to a careful study of the Bible. As he agonized over it day after day, he came to an understanding that transformed his life and, through the Protestant Reformation, transformed the world. He came to see for himself that the Bible truly is "living and abiding" (1 Peter 1:23). The Bible has life and the Bible brings life because it has been spoken by God. The Bible's life, its voice, its feet, and hands are the life, voice, feet, and hands of God extended toward his people. For that reason among others it is always worthy of our time, our attention, and our dedication. Have you read your Bible today?

WE FIND CHRIST
IN ALL THE SCRIPTURES.
IN THE OLD TESTAMENT HE IS
PREDICTED, IN THE GOSPELS HE
IS REVEALED, IN ACTS HE IS
PREACHED, IN THE EPISTLES
HE IS EXPLAINED, AND IN
REVELATION HE IS
EXPECTED.

Alistair Begg

The Bible is, by its very nature, a collection—a collection of histories, biographies, letters, prophecies, and poetry written across about 1,500 years in many different settings and many different cultures. You might wonder, why these books and why not others? What binds together the sixty-six books that together make up *the* book is that they are the complete and authoritative collection of *inspired* writings—writings that came to humanity from the mind of God. This being the case, we would expect there to be a kind of unity even amid all the diversity of authors, settings, contexts, and cultures. And sure enough, this is exactly what we find and exactly what Alistair Begg wants us to see. The unifying theme of the Bible is Jesus Christ (Luke 24:27). In the Old Testament writings he is predicted and longed for. In the Gospels he is revealed and described. In the book of Acts he is preached, in the epistles (letters) he is explained, and in the final book, the book of Revelation, he is expected to make his grand return. In this way, Jesus is the theme of the Bible and is present on every page.

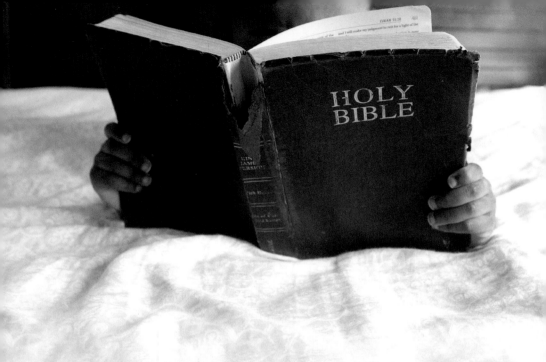

A Bible that's falling apart usually belongs to someone who *isn't*.

UNKNOWN

We have entered into an age where many people are leaving behind their printed Bibles in favor of digital equivalents. Any new technology introduces both benefits and drawbacks, and while there are many wonderful features that come with our digital Bibles, there is this downside: Our Bibles are no longer a visible demonstration of our commitment to God's Word. It has long been the case that some of the holiest people own some of the most tattered Bibles. Placed on the gleaming wooden coffin of many a precious saint has been a Bible whose cover is worn, whose pages are falling out, whose margins are scrawled with lead and ink. As these people committed themselves to God's Word day after day, as they carried their Bible to church week after week, as they read it and marked it and integrated it into their mornings and evenings, it began to show inevitable wear and tear. And as they went to be with the Lord, they left it behind as a precious artifact that attested to their love for the Lord and their long labor in his Word. As that Bible grew ever more beat-up, their soul grew ever more cleaned up.

MARK IT DOWN
—YOUR PROGRESS IN HOLINESS WILL
NEVER EXCEED YOUR RELATIONSHIP
WITH THE HOLY WORD OF GOD.

Nancy DeMoss Wolgemuth

Sometimes in life we puzzle over God's will for us. Sometimes we have to make momentous decisions that may alter the course of our lives and the course of other people's. In those moments we may scour the Bible looking for something, anything, to direct our way; something, anything, to give us confidence that we know and can do the will of God. But at its most basic level, the will of God for our lives is very simple. God wishes for us to be like him, which is to say, God wishes for us to be holy. "As he who called you is holy, you also be holy in all your conduct" (1 Peter 1:15). And it is in the Bible that God has revealed how we can live holy and upright lives. This puts the onus on each of us to make a careful, deliberate, and ongoing study of the Bible, for as Nancy DeMoss Wolgemuth says, "Your progress in holiness will never exceed your relationship with the holy Word of God." Mark it down—the holiest Christians are also the "Bibleiest" Christians.

Spiritual growth depends on two things:

1st   a willingness to live according to the Word of God;

2nd   a willingness to take whatever consequences emerge as a result.

Sinclair Ferguson

Christianity is a religion of faith—we must put our faith in the Lord Jesus Christ, "for by grace you have been saved through faith. And this is not your own doing; it is the gift of God" (Ephesians 2:8). In faith we rest in Christ, trusting that his work and not our own has brought reconciliation between man and God. And while there must be a one-time act in which we express faith in him, faith is also an ongoing reality in which we trust that God's ways are better than our ways, and that God's instructions direct us to the truest and best ways to live. Thus Sinclair Ferguson says that to be Christians who are thriving and growing, we must have "a willingness to live according to the Word of God." But there is more to the equation. We must also have "a willingness to take whatever consequences emerge as a result." We put our faith in Christ to be saved and then enter into a lifetime of faith, a lifetime of trusting that God's ways are higher than our ways and his thoughts than our thoughts (Isaiah 55:9).

Nowhere does the Bible command a daily "quiet time." Yet often does the Bible commend an earnest commitment to reading the Bible, meditating upon it, and diligently applying its truths. Often does it commend those who lived according to it. David's passion should be all of ours: "Oh how I love your law! It is my meditation all the day" (Psalm 119:97). Josiah's commitment should be that of every Christian—when he rediscovered the Bible after it had been lost, he "made a covenant before the LORD, to walk after the LORD and to keep his commandments and his testimonies and his statutes with all his heart and all his soul, to perform the words of this covenant that were written in this book" (2 Kings 23:3). To fail in our commitment to the Bible is to fail in our commitment to know and honor and obey God himself, for the Bible is *his* Word, *his* law, *his* truth. It is *his* lamp meant to guide our feet and *his* light meant to illume the way we must go (Psalm 119:105). Though sin may keep us from the Bible, the Bible will keep us from sin if only we commit ourselves to it.

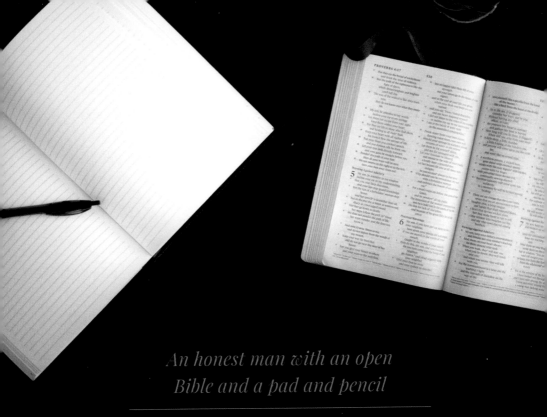

*An honest man with an open
Bible and a pad and pencil*

is sure to find out what is wrong
with him very quickly.

A.W. TOZER

In Psalm 19, David describes God's "two books"—the book of nature, through which God is speaking of his existence, power, and glory, and the book of Scripture, through which he provides much more extensive knowledge of his works and ways. David was committed to making a close study of both of these forms of revelation and kept a "pad and pencil" at hand so he could reflect on them. The words he jotted down became the words of this wonderful psalm. His close study of God's revelation led to the concluding verses of the psalm, where David prays that God will show him his sins and faults, that God would motivate him to live a blameless and innocent life. Tozer says that "an honest man with an open Bible and a pad and pencil is sure to find out what is wrong with him very quickly," and Psalm 19 provides a clear example from the life of David. His closing words are a prayer for each of us: "Let the words of my mouth and the meditation of my heart be acceptable in your sight, O Lord, my rock and my redeemer" (Psalm 19:14).

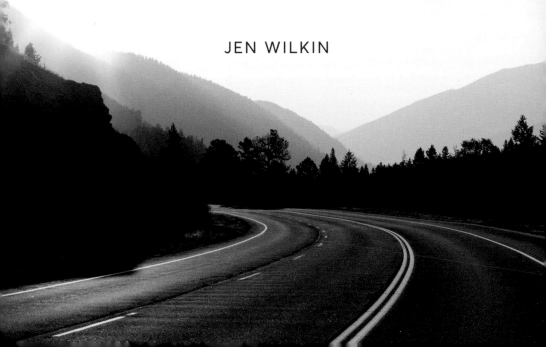

We will not wake up ten years from now and find we have passively taken on the character of God.

JEN WILKIN

God calls us to live lives marked by holiness. God could have arranged the world in such a way that when we put our faith in Christ, he immediately "zaps" us with the full measure of holy character. But instead he has called us to a lifetime of laboring toward it. He has called us to diligently put off every sinful thought, desire, and behavior and to deliberately put on the full measure of righteousness. He calls us to "strive...for the holiness without which no one will see the Lord" (Hebrews 12:14). To strive is to make a great effort toward a goal or achievement. It is to labor, to strain, to toil, to work incessantly to attain victory. "We will not wake up ten years from now and find we have passively taken on the character of God." That is impossible and unrealistic. It is sinful and lazy. If we wish to have the character of God, we must apply ourselves to the Word and allow it to shape and mold us until we are conformed to his image. What a wonderful and noble goal! And what a fitting reward for our labor.

UNLIKE ANY OTHER BOOK
THAT HAS EVER BEEN WRITTEN,

the Bible is alive;

& IT COMES WITH A PERSONAL TUTOR

–the Holy Spirit,

WHO LIVES IN US.

*Nancy Leigh
DeMoss*

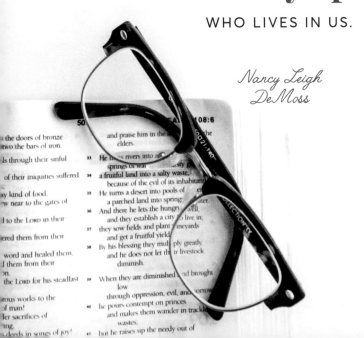

The Bible is unique among all books in that it is living and active. "You received the word of God, which you heard from us...," says Paul to one of his churches, "not as the word of men but as what it really is, the word of God, *which is at work in you believers*" (1 Thessalonians 2:13). The Bible is living and working within believers because of the unique ministry of the Holy Spirit. Before his ascension, Jesus promised that "when the Spirit of truth comes, he will guide you into all the truth" (John 16:13). In fact, what the Spirit would bring is so good and so important that Jesus could actually say, "It is to your advantage that I go away, for if I do not go away, the Helper will not come to you" (John 16:7). The promised Spirit has come, and one of the great helps this Helper performs is a kind of tutoring. After taking up residence within us, he illumines the truths of the Bible to our minds and hearts so we can understand them and so we can do them.

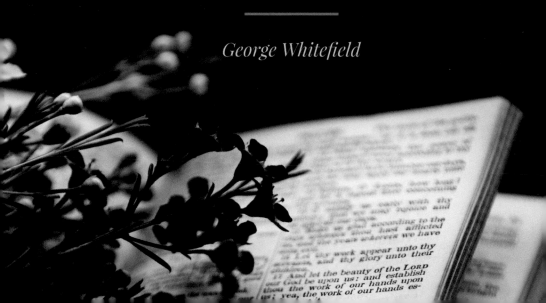

God has condescended to become an author,

AND YET PEOPLE WILL NOT READ HIS WRITINGS.

There are very few that ever gave this Book of God,

THE GRAND CHARTER OF SALVATION,

one fair reading through.

———

George Whitefield

Perhaps the most remarkable characteristic of our God is his willingness to condescend to us. Out of love for his people he will bestow the most unexpected gifts and take the most unexpected actions—even ones that seem far below the dignity of a God who is "holy, holy, holy" (Isaiah 6:3; Revelation 4:8). We see this most notably in the willingness of Jesus to take on human flesh and then to humble himself "by becoming obedient to the point of death, even death on a cross" (Philippians 2:8). But we see it as well in God's willingness to become an author, to give us this record of his acts and his deeds, his purposes and his promises. And yet, though this omniscient, eternal, and holy God has given us his writings, and though through the Bible he has revealed the way we can be saved, few take the time to give it a fair reading, and few bother to read it all the way through. Christian, receive this book as a gift and commit yourself to reading its broad story and its fine details, for both tell the story of God's amazing grace.

If you find a professing Christian **indifferent to his Bible,** you may be sure that the very dust upon its cover will rise up in **judgment against him.**

C.H. Spurgeon

Hank Williams recorded an old song called "Dust on the Bible." It's a song of lament in which he has gone to a friend's home and asked to see their Bible. When they bring it to him, he realizes it has obviously not been read for a very long time, for it is covered in dust. "Oh, you can read your magazines of love and tragic things / But not one word of Bible verse, not a Scripture do you know / When it is the very truth and its contents good for you / But if dust is covered o'er it / it is sure to doom your soul."

Perhaps Williams had encountered this quote by Charles Spurgeon, who wants us to consider that there is a terrible disconnect between a profession of Christian faith and an apathetic disposition toward the Bible. While we may all go through lulls when for a time we may drift from our commitment to the Bible, the true Christian will always return to it, for to neglect it is to imperil our very lives. It is food for our souls, it is light for our eyes, it is enlightenment for our hearts. We cannot live and we cannot thrive without it.

READING GIVES US BREADTH, BUT STUDY GIVES US DEPTH.

[JERRY BRIDGES]

One of the key principles of properly understanding and applying the Bible is this: Scripture interprets Scripture. Christians sometimes speak of "the analogy of faith" to express the fact that we have properly understood one part of the Bible only when we have interpreted it in the context of the whole Bible. This puts the call on each of us to know the Bible both deeply and widely. While it is right and good to emphasize the importance of meditation, of slowly pondering a single verse or a single truth, it is also important that we have some understanding of the entire book. This is why we must sometimes read quickly and other times read slowly. This is why there is benefit in reading the entire Bible rapidly and repeatedly and why there is benefit in reading it slowly and meditatively. Reading and rereading the Bible gives us breadth of knowledge, while studying and pondering it gives us depth of understanding. Neither is superior to the other. In fact, both are crucial, for the Bible is its own interpreter.

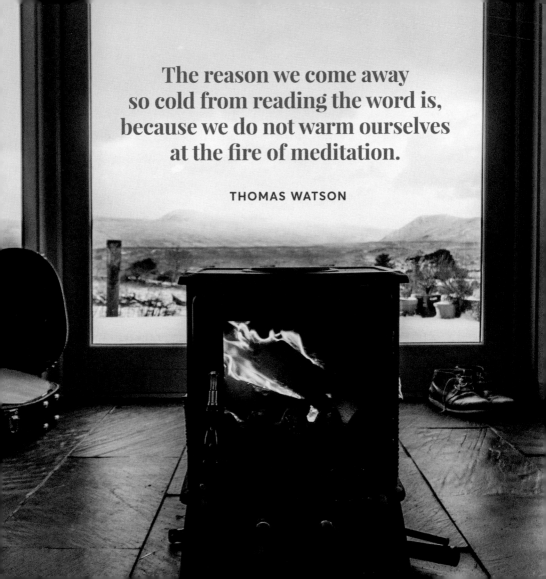

The reason we come away
so cold from reading the word is,
because we do not warm ourselves
at the fire of meditation.

THOMAS WATSON

We live at a time in which we are constantly inundated with information. We live much of our lives within the glow of digital devices that are constantly beeping, buzzing, and flashing to tell us there is new information available to be had—text messages, emails, tweets, headlines. But in such a context, it is important to understand the distinction between information and wisdom. Where information is mere facts and figures, wisdom is the application of those facts and figures to real life. Man shall not and cannot live by information alone! He must live by wisdom. "The beginning of wisdom is this: Get wisdom, and whatever you get, get insight" (Proverbs 4:7). If we are not careful, we can read our Bibles like we read the news—as a means to gain facts but not as a means to grow in wisdom. Thomas Watson reminds us that simply reading the Bible is not enough, for mere facts will do us little good. We must slowly ponder it, we must diligently apply ourselves to it, we must let ourselves meditate upon it until we have grown not only in information but in wisdom.

MEDITATION IS THE ACTIVITY OF CALLING TO MIND,

AND THINKING OVER, AND DWELLING ON,

AND APPLYING TO ONESELF, THE VARIOUS THINGS

THAT ONE KNOWS ABOUT THE WORKS AND WAYS

AND PURPOSES AND PROMISES OF GOD.

J.I. PACKER

Thomas Watson warns that "the reason we come away so cold from reading the word is, because we do not warm ourselves at the fire of meditation." So what is this meditation that he deems so important? It is crucial we distinguish it from a fraudulent form that is increasingly popular today. Christians are not to engage in the meditation of Eastern religions that involves emptying the mind that it may be filled with a kind of self-knowledge. Rather, the meditation the Bible commends involves filling the mind to achieve knowledge of God. It is the meditation of Psalm 1:1-2: "Blessed is the man who walks not in the counsel of the wicked, nor stands in the way of sinners, nor sits in the seat of scoffers; but his delight is in the law of the LORD, and on his law he meditates day and night." To meditate in this way is to call to mind the great truths God reveals about himself—his works and ways and purposes and promises—and then to think about them, to ponder them, to prayerfully consider them, to allow the mind to dwell on them. Just as heat sets the soft clay to become hard bricks, meditation fixes the truths of Scripture within our hearts, our minds, our lives.

LET US LABOR TO MEMORIZE THE

WORD OF GOD—FOR WORSHIP AND FOR WARFARE.

IF WE DO NOT CARRY IT IN OUR HEADS,

WE CANNOT SAVOR IT IN OUR HEARTS

OR WIELD IT IN THE SPIRIT.

John Piper

We are an educated people with high standards of literacy. We are a free people who enjoy religious liberty. We are a wealthy people with unlimited access to a nearly infinite quantity of Bibles. We are a privileged people who may not realize how blessed we are. Many of our forebears and even many of our contemporaries have not been capable of reading the Bible, have not had the liberty to read it, and have not had access to it. To be able to know and apply the Bible, they have had to memorize it. And while it is right that we enjoy all our privileges and all our liberties, they may foster a kind of spiritual laziness in which we consider the Bible on our shelves as good as the Bible in our mind. John Piper puts out the call even to us to be diligent in memorizing it, for "if we do not carry it in our heads, we cannot savor it in our hearts or wield it in the Spirit." To memorize the Bible is to put the best thing in the best place for the best reason! It is effort that will bear fruit in every life.

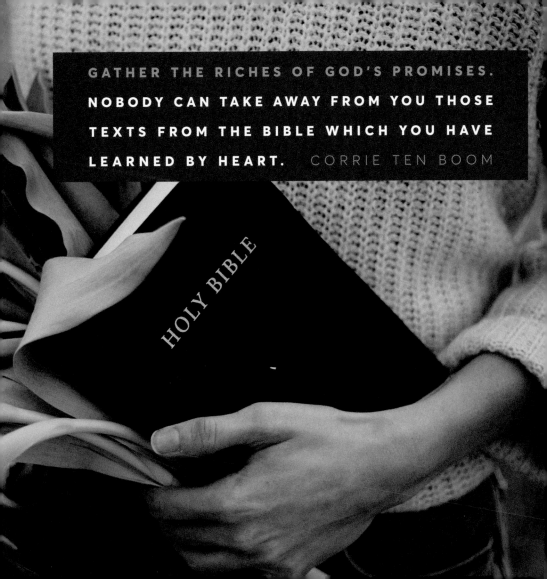

GATHER THE RICHES OF GOD'S PROMISES. NOBODY CAN TAKE AWAY FROM YOU THOSE TEXTS FROM THE BIBLE WHICH YOU HAVE LEARNED BY HEART. CORRIE TEN BOOM

Corrie ten Boom knew what it was to suffer deprivation, to have to do without so many of life's luxuries and even its necessities. Arrested and sent to a concentration camp for her role in sheltering Jews from the Nazis, she spent almost a year in confinement and suffered the loss of her father and sister. But her faith remained intact and unmoved. It was in those days of such trial that she relied upon the riches she had accumulated through a lifetime of following Jesus. From the time she was a child, she had read God's Word and set its truths deep into her mind and heart. Now, as she suffered, she could call those truths to mind, meditate on them, and trust in them. While the German army could take every one of her possessions from her, they could not take those truths. When she had nothing else to sustain her, she had the rich promises of God. And so can you, if only you will learn them by heart.

IT IS A GOOD THING TO BE A STUDENT OF THE WORD, BUT ONLY IN ORDER TO BE A PRACTISER & EXPERIENCER OF THE WORD.

D. Martyn Lloyd-Jones

Motives matter, even (or perhaps especially) when it comes to something as very good as studying the Bible. The best motive for reading the Bible is to be transformed by it. For this to happen, we must approach our reading and studying with both confidence and humility, asking God to transform us through his Word. Many skeptics read the Bible for a very different purpose—so they can attack it or undermine it, so they can disprove it or mock it. They prove that great knowledge of the Bible may actually lead them farther from God, all because their motives have been wrong. But even Christians can read the Bible for ignoble purposes, perhaps so they can content themselves that they have more knowledge of it than someone else, or perhaps so they can feel like they have crossed off that box on their daily list of tasks. As Lloyd-Jones reminds us, our efforts in the Word should always be leading toward wisdom, which is living a life that is fully pleasing to God. It is good to be a student of the Bible, but only if we are studying for the right reason—to practice and experience it in our daily lives.

Whenever a man takes upon him
to make additions to the Scriptures,

he is likely to end with valuing his
own additions above Scripture itself.

J.C. RYLE

Humanity's plunge into sin came when the first human beings failed to take God's words seriously. God had clearly revealed his will to them, but they doubted it, they challenged it, they defied it. The account of the Fall is a sober warning to each of us that God's Word is always true and that we must always obey it. Many books, chapters, and verses later we come to the end of the Bible and this sober warning:

"I warn everyone who hears the words of the prophecy of this book: if anyone adds to them, God will add to him the plagues described in this book, and if anyone takes away from the words of the book of this prophecy, God will take away his share in the tree of life and in the holy city, which are described in this book (Revelation 22:18-19)."

If the Bible is so good and true and complete, why would we ever add to it or take away from it? Ryle hints at it here: We would do so only because we prefer our own wisdom ahead of God's. But the Bible itself often attests to the deadly danger this represents.

THE ONLY REVELATION
FROM GOD WHICH
CHRISTIANS STILL AWAIT IS
THE REVELATION OF JESUS
CHRIST AT HIS SECOND
COMING.

Geoffrey B. Wilson

If for so many centuries God revealed himself through the inspired writings that make up the Bible, is it possible that he may add more inspired writings today or in the future? It is a fair question and forces us to distinguish between what God can do and what God has said he will do. God has the ability to reveal himself in whatever ways he wants. If he so desired, he could inspire more authors to write more Scriptures. But in the final book of the Bible, God makes it clear that it represents the end of this kind of revelation (see Revelation 22:18-19). The Bible, then, is a "closed canon." A canon is an authoritative collection of any author's work; it is open as long as the author is adding to it, and closed when he has written his final word. In this case the author is God, and he has indeed written the last word he intends to write. But that does not mean he has finished with all revelation of himself. To the contrary, the greatest of all revelations, the greatest of all revealings, is still to come. We eagerly await the revelation of Jesus Christ at his second coming!

The Bible was given to bear witness
to one God, Creator and Sustainer of the
universe, through Christ, Redeemer of sinful man.

**IT PRESENTS ONE CONTINUOUS STORY
–THAT OF HUMAN REDEMPTION.**

Merrill Unger

The Bible is a story made up of many stories, a grand narrative made up of many smaller narratives. From Genesis to Revelation, from Old Testament to New Testament, from histories to prophecies, it tells one big story and ultimately bears witness to the existence, the providence, and the redemptive work of one great God. Its four major plot points are Creation, in which God made the world good and perfect; Fall, in which humanity rebelled against God and brought evil into the world; Redemption, in which God entered the world in the person of Jesus Christ to redeem his people from their sin; and Restoration, which tells of the coming day when Christ will return to judge sin, eradicate evil, and usher in a never-ending era of perfect peace. Whenever we read the Bible we must always orient ourselves within this narrative, for it is the Bible's story, God's story, and ultimately our story. We cannot know and understand ourselves and we cannot know and understand our God if we do not know and understand the story the Bible tells.

The great cause of neglecting the Scriptures is not want of time, but want of heart, some idol taking the place of Christ.

Robert Chapman

Many Christians experience a contradiction between what we believe to be true about the Bible and our actual practice of reading the Bible. Often our theology is superior to our habits. We profess that the Bible is infallible, inerrant, authoritative, and sufficient, but we then neglect it in our daily lives. We agree with David when he says of God's words, "More to be desired are they than gold, even much fine gold; sweeter also than honey and drippings of the honeycomb" (Psalm 19:10). Yet in our lives we show little hunger for those good, pure, sweet, nourishing words. How can this be? It is because we allow other things to take the place that should be reserved for God and his Word. It is not that we lack time, but that we lack desire. It is not that we lack ability, but that we lack interest. We allow some idol, something that displaces in our lives the place of prominence that only God deserves. Whether it is entertainment, work, socializing, or something else altogether, we will not prioritize God until we uproot that idol.

Men do not reject the Bible because it contradicts itself, but because it contradicts them.

E. PAUL HOVEY

There is an entire sector of the publishing industry that is dedicated to undermining people's confidence in the Bible. Many of these books shoot to the top of the bestseller lists with their novel conspiracies about the Bible's origins, their theories about its hidden secrets, or their conviction that it is a mess of contradictions. And indeed, a cursory reading of the Bible will quickly turn up what appear to be contradictions. "Answer not a fool according to his folly, lest you be like him yourself," says Proverbs 26:4. Yet in the very next verse we read, "Answer a fool according to his folly, lest he be wise in his own eyes." But those who wrote the Bible were no fools. They knew what God had said in the past and, guided by the Holy Spirit, made no mistakes, introduced no conflicts. So while some people insist they have rejected the Bible because of its incoherence, E. Paul Hovey offers a profound insight when he says, "Men do not reject the Bible because it contradicts itself, but because it contradicts them." Their real beef is with what the Bible says about them and what it calls them to.

We *must quit bending*
the Word to suit our situation.
It is we who must be bent to that Word,
our necks that must bow under the yoke.

———

Elisabeth Elliot

As Christians we are people of the Word, people who live according to the Bible. To live according to the Bible we must properly understand the Bible, and this demands reading it carefully and interpreting it correctly. While the Bible can at times be difficult, we can have confidence that the Holy Spirit will guide us as we prayerfully pursue the truth God has revealed in his Word (John 16:12-13). We must always pray that we would conform ourselves to the Word rather than conforming the Word to ourselves. We must always pray that we would allow our desires to be changed according to the Bible rather than allowing the Bible to be changed according to our desires. We must guard ourselves against looking to the Bible for confirmation of our longings rather than looking to the Bible for truth that may contradict our longings. As Elisabeth Elliot warns, we must stop bending the Bible to suit our situation, but rather bend ourselves to suit the Word. We must humble ourselves and pray with David, "Search me, O God, and know my heart! Try me and know my thoughts! And see if there be any grievous way in me, and lead me in the way everlasting!" (Psalm 139:23-24).

Nothing less than a whole Bible
CAN MAKE A WHOLE CHRISTIAN.

A.W. Tozer

The Bible is a canon, an authoritative collection of one author's works. In this case, the author is God, and he has given us sixty-six books, each one unique and each one serving a distinct purpose. Each book was inspired by God's Spirit and reveals God's mind and God's plan, yet most Christians spend the great majority of their time reading only a few—perhaps Genesis and Psalms from the Old Testament and the Gospels and the letters of Paul from the New. Much of the Bible, or even most of it, goes unread. Few dare to plunge into the unusual laws and regulations of Leviticus, the troubling histories of Judges, the long prophecies of Isaiah and Ezekiel. Yet if each of these books is from God and ultimately about God, then each book teaches us how we can best honor God. "Nothing less than a whole Bible can make a whole Christian." That being true, a partial Bible makes only a partial Christian. Make it your habit to read not some, but all of God's Word, for every book, every chapter, every verse has treasures to uncover! "Man shall not live by bread alone, but by *every* word that comes from the mouth of God" (Matthew 4:4).

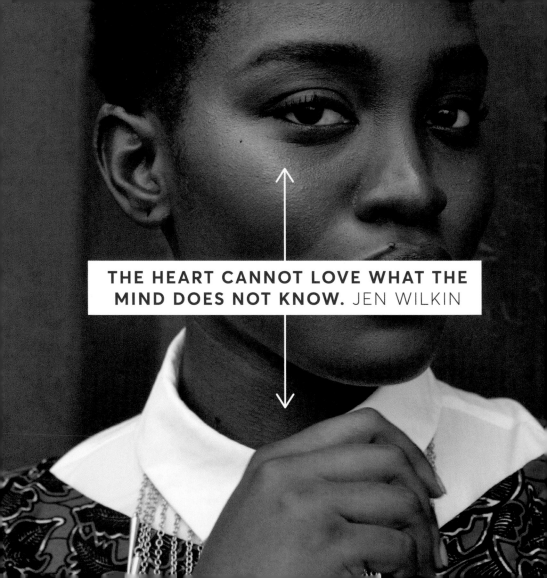

THE HEART CANNOT LOVE WHAT THE MIND DOES NOT KNOW. JEN WILKIN

In his letter to the church at Rome, the apostle Paul expresses his sorrow about some people who were zealously religious yet tragically misguided. "I bear them witness that they have a zeal for God," he says, "but not according to knowledge" (Romans 10:2). Though these people were acting in ways that seemed to mark the very pinnacle of religious devotion, they were actually acting in ways that were contrary to God's Word. Why? Because what they believed to be true about God was actually false. For that reason the actions they took out of devotion to God actually contradicted the will of God. They were zealous but ignorant. And what was true of them can be true of us. We, too, can serve a God of our own imagining rather than the God who actually is. Thus in order to rightly worship God, we must first rightly know God. We must apply ourselves to knowing God as he reveals himself so our zeal for him is based on knowledge rather than ignorance. For, to echo Wilkin, the heart cannot properly and truly love what the mind does not know.

WE SPEAK

Relationships depend upon speaking and listening, upon knowing and being known. This is true of every one of our human relationships and equally true of our relationship with God. While God speaks to us through the Bible, we speak to him through prayer. Just as God shares his mind and heart with us through his Word, we share our minds and hearts with him as we pray. He speaks and we listen; we speak and he listens. It is nothing short of a wonder that created beings like you and me can have a genuine, living, ongoing relationship with the Creator of the universe.

This section is a collection of quotes that focus on the wonder of prayer, the practice of prayer, the discipline of prayer, the joy of prayer, and the expectations we can have as we pray to our God, our Father, our Friend.

The men who have
done the most for God
in this world have been
early on their knees.

E.M. BOUNDS

This quote would work perfectly well without the word "early." "The men who have done the most for God in this world have been on their knees." Taken that way, it would cause us to reflect on the close connection between prayer and a biblical view of productivity—doing good for others to the glory of God. We could then point to the prayer habits of Jesus or the apostle Paul, both of whom prayed constantly and did so much for God in this world. But Bounds *did* include the word "early" because he wanted to call Christians not only to pray, but to make prayer the day's first priority. Here is how he continues his thought: "He who fritters away the early morning, its opportunity and freshness, in other pursuits than seeking God will make poor headway seeking Him the rest of the day." While the Bible does not command we pray early in the day, doing so is certainly the one sure way to ensure that life's busyness does not displace prayer. Bounds adds, "If God is not first in our thoughts and efforts in the morning, He will be in the last place the remainder of the day."

Don't pray when you feel like it. Have an appointment with the Lord & keep it. A man is powerful on his knees.

CORRIE TEN BOOM

In Jesus Christ, we have a great High Priest who stands always ready to make intercession between us and the Father. "Let us then with confidence draw near to the throne of grace, that we may receive mercy and find grace to help in time of need" (Hebrews 4:16). We can at any moment cry out to God in prayer and be confident that he hears us. We can pray whenever we feel like it and whenever we feel we need it. Yet this is not enough, for we need God's help not only when we feel the need for it—we need his help every moment of every day. As the hymnwriter Annie Sherwood Hawks wrote in 1872, "I need thee, oh, I need thee; / Every hour I need thee! / Oh, bless me now, my Savior; / I come to thee."

For this reason we should build habits of prayer and then be disciplined in maintaining those habits. Pray spontaneously, but not only spontaneously. "Have an appointment with the Lord and keep it," says Corrie ten Boom, for "a man is powerful on his knees."

PRAYER IS *NOT* LIKE A GOOD RECIPE:

SIMPLY FOLLOW A SET OF MECHANICAL
DIRECTIONS AND EVERYTHING
TURNS OUT RIGHT IN THE END.

D.A. Carson

Though in the Lord's Prayer Jesus provided a basic structure to inform the way we pray, he did not provide a formula. And in fact, no such formula exists, for prayer is not meant to be formulaic. It is not meant to be an exercise in rote statements or vain repetitions. "Prayer is not like a good recipe," says D.A. Carson, in which you "simply follow a set of mechanical directions and everything turns out right in the end." So what is prayer? Perhaps no one has defined it better than John Bunyan: "Prayer is a sincere, sensible, affectionate pouring out of the heart or soul to God, through Christ, in the strength and assistance of the Holy Spirit, for such things as God has promised, or according to the Word of God, for the good of the church, with submission in faith to the will of God."[5] Thus we can, should, and must pray from the heart and pray earnestly, knowing and trusting that God hears and God responds to the prayers of his saints.

Prayer is **not** learned in a classroom **but** in the closet.

E.M. Bounds

Christians are well-resourced with tremendous books that teach the theology and the practice of prayer (including the classic works on prayer by E.M. Bounds, the author of this quote). Many churches and ministries offer powerful classes that teach why we must pray and how we must pray. But as Bounds tells us here, the best place to learn prayer is not a classroom, but a closet. The best way to learn prayer is not to read books on prayer, but to simply pray. The books and classes can help, to be sure. But at some point we must simply close our eyes and pray. Even with our lack of confidence, even with our lack of knowledge, even with our lack of theology, we must simply close our eyes and open our mouths and speak to God. And as we commit ourselves to the discipline of prayer, as we engage in it day after day and year after year, we find ourselves learning what it means to pray with faith, with power, with humility, with persistence. Christian, if you want to learn to pray, pray!

Many pray with their **lips** for that for which their **hearts** have no desire.

Jonathan Edwards

It is no great feat to convince another person of a lie. Because other people cannot see our inner selves, they are easily deceived. But as we pray to God, we pray to one who knows our innermost thoughts, our innermost desires, our innermost longings. We pray to one who knows us far better than we know ourselves. He weighs the heart (Proverbs 21:2), he knows the heart (1 Samuel 16:7), he searches the heart (Jeremiah 17:10), he observes the secrets of the heart (Psalm 44:21), and he even discerns the thoughts and intentions of the heart (Hebrews 4:12). Nothing is hidden from his sight. Rather, "all are naked and exposed to the eyes of him to whom we must give account" (Hebrews 4:13). That being the case, we ought to pray with honesty. We ought to put aside any thoughts of deceiving God or being less than honest with God. There is no benefit to mouthing words that do not reflect our hearts. But there is great benefit in honestly telling God our every struggle, our every temptation, our every desire, and asking him to extend to us his grace, his mercy.

THE THINGS
YOU PRAY ABOUT ARE THE
THINGS YOU TRUST GOD TO HANDLE.
THE THINGS YOU NEGLECT TO PRAY
ABOUT ARE THE THINGS YOU TRUST
YOU CAN HANDLE ON YOUR OWN.

H.B. Charles Jr.

There is a close connection between prayer and humility. This being the case, there is also a close connection between prayerlessness and pride. Those who believe they are self-sufficient feel no need to petition God for his help, for his strength, for his wisdom. It is only those who admit their lack who will cry out to God. H.B. Charles lays out a sobering challenge: "The things you pray about are the things you trust God to handle." Conversely, "the things you neglect to pray about are the things you trust you can handle on your own." In this way both prayer and prayerlessness are deeply significant and even deeply symbolic. To pray is to admit we need help; to fail to pray is to indicate we feel no need for help. Is there any area of life in which we need no divine help whatsoever? Of course not! Then there is no area of life we should not pray about; there is no petition too small. We can, we must, make our requests known to God.

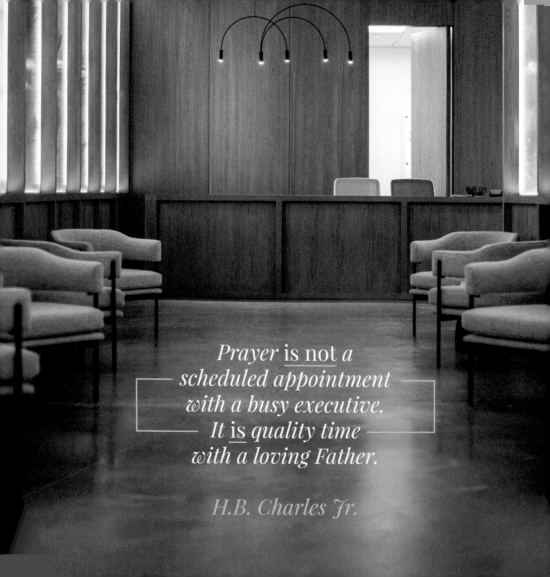

Prayer is not *a*
scheduled appointment
with a busy executive.
It is *quality time*
with a loving Father.

H.B. Charles Jr.

People of all faiths pray. Some pray to gods, some to ancestors, some to nature, and some to the universe, but all speak out words, all utter desires, all hope to be heard. But Christians pray differently and Christians pray confidently, for we pray to a Father. We alone "have received the Spirit of adoption as sons, by whom we cry, 'Abba! Father!'" (Romans 8:15). Jesus taught us to begin our prayers with the precious words "Our Father." This changes everything about the way we pray, for we are not appealing to an impersonal universe or a powerless rock. We are not appealing to an ancestor who has already lived and died and returned to the dust. We are not appealing to a deity who is cold and indifferent to us. We are not appealing to a god who has no interest and no time. Rather, we are spending quality time with a Father—a gracious Father who "in love...predestined us for adoption to himself as sons through Jesus Christ, according to the purpose of his will, to the praise of his glorious grace" (Ephesians 1:4-6).

We have to pray with our eyes on God,

NOT ON THE DIFFICULTIES.

Oswald Chambers

Life inevitably faces us with grievous trials and terrible troubles. None of us remains unscathed and undamaged as we make our way through this fallen world. When trials come, they can loom up so large before us that they become the only thing we can see. And even if we find the strength to cry out to God, we cry out with our gaze fixed on the difficulty—on the disease, the loss, the temptation, the pandemic, the financial fears. It is in this context that Oswald Chambers exhorts us to shift our gaze to something bigger, something stronger, something more permanent than our trial. "We have to pray with our eyes on God, not on the difficulties." We see this perfectly modeled in Jesus Christ, who, with the specter of the cross looming before him, said to his disciples, "'My soul is very sorrowful, even to death; remain here, and watch with me.' And going a little farther he fell on his face and prayed" (Matthew 26:38-39). In the deepest agony of spirit, with the darkest trial before him, he set his eyes on the Father. Shouldn't we do the same?

We must wrestle earnestly in prayer,

LIKE MEN CONTENDING WITH A DEADLY ENEMY FOR LIFE.

J.C. Ryle

One of the most poignant of Jesus's parables tells the story of a persistent widow. Having faced injustice at the hand of an adversary, this woman appealed to the local judge. She asked him to use his power and authority to right the wrong that had been done to her. But to her sorrow, she learned this was an unjust judge who did not care to help her. Still, she returned to him again and again, she made appeal after appeal, until she wore him out. Eventually, if only to preserve his own sanity, the judge relented and responded to her pleas. Jesus wanted his hearers to make a comparison from the lesser to the greater. If even an unjust and uncaring judge will eventually grant the pleas of someone he dislikes, how much more will a just and caring Father grant the pleas of the child he loves? Luke explains the moral of the story: We "ought always to pray and not lose heart" (Luke 18:1). And so Ryle can rightly say, "We must wrestle earnestly in prayer." And though we wrestle as if we are contending with a deadly enemy, we are actually making our petitions to a loving God.

Prayer is not eloquence, *but earnestness;*
not the definition of helplessness, *but the feeling of it;*
not figures of speech, *but earnestness of soul.*

HANNAH MORE

When Jesus's disciples asked for instruction on prayer, he warned them of a common temptation—the temptation to think that prayer depends upon saying just the right words or a certain number of words. "When you pray, do not heap up empty phrases as the Gentiles do, for they think that they will be heard for their many words. Do not be like them, for your Father knows what you need before you ask him" (Matthew 6:7-8). When we pray to God, our foremost concern should not be the quantity of our words or even the quality of our words. Rather, our concern should be the purity of our hearts and the earnestness of our souls. God cares little for our eloquence but cares a great deal for our humility and sincerity. When you pray, whether privately or with others, it is far better to pray with the innocence and simplicity of a child than to pray with the arrogance and eloquence of a Pharisee.

Any concern too small to be turned into a prayer
IS TOO SMALL TO BE MADE INTO A BURDEN.

Corrie ten Boom

At times we all live burdened lives, weighed down by the cares and concerns, the trials and traumas that inevitably accompany life in this world. And while we sometimes feel crushed by life's heaviest burdens—the death of a loved one, the rebellion of a child, the onset of a chronic illness—we can also sometimes stagger under the weight of the relentless accumulation of many smaller burdens. In our times of difficulty we need to remember that Psalm 55:22 says, "Cast your burden on the LORD, and he will sustain you; he will never permit the righteous to be moved." God is willing and able to help us, so through prayer we can and should throw our burdens on his shoulders. But with all the great sorrows in the world and in our lives, does he have time and patience for the lesser ones? He does! If it is big enough to be a concern for us, it is big enough to be a concern for him. Or as Corrie ten Boom reminds us, "Any concern too small to be turned into a prayer is too small to be made into a burden."

Spread out your petition before God,
and then say, "Thy will, not mine, be done."

———

THE SWEETEST LESSON I HAVE LEARNED IN GOD'S SCHOOL

IS TO LET THE LORD CHOOSE FOR ME.

D.L. Moody

Though we are limited beings with little knowledge, we are proud beings with little humility. When Jesus taught us to pray, he taught us to bring our petitions before the Lord, to bring to him all our cares, all our burdens, all our sorrows. We can and should plead our case before the Lord, for Jesus tells us, "If you then, who are evil, know how to give good gifts to your children, how much more will your Father who is in heaven give good things to those who ask him!" (Matthew 7:11). Yet we need to do so humbly, acknowledging that God may have purposes in mind that he has not yet made clear to us. And so when we pray and when we bring our requests to the Lord, we say, "Your will be done, on earth as it is in heaven" (Matthew 6:10). In these words we acknowledge what God has made clear: "As the heavens are higher than the earth, so are my ways higher than your ways and my thoughts than your thoughts" (Isaiah 55:9). We humbly, willingly submit to the choices of the God who is working all things for our good and his glory.

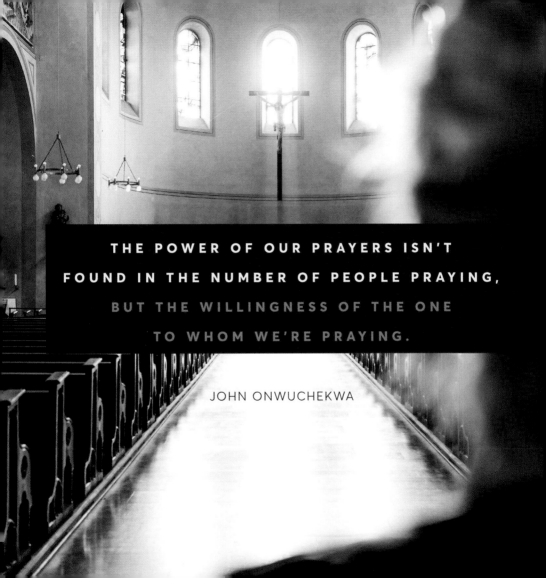

THE POWER OF OUR PRAYERS ISN'T
FOUND IN THE NUMBER OF PEOPLE PRAYING,
BUT THE WILLINGNESS OF THE ONE
TO WHOM WE'RE PRAYING.

JOHN ONWUCHEKWA

There are times when we pray out of a sense of desperation, times when we know that all we can do is pray. And so we may put out the call to friends, to family, to the local church, or to the public: Please pray! This is the right thing to do, for God loves to hear the prayers of his people. Yet even here we must guard ourselves against thinking that God will be more willing to hear the prayers of many people than to hear the prayer of one. Whether we are on our knees alone and unseen, or assembling with an entire congregation, or putting out the appeal to the whole world through social media, the comfort we find is the same: that God loves to hear our prayers and to respond to our prayers. Ultimately, as John Onwuchekwa reminds us, "The power of our prayers isn't found in the number of people praying, but the willingness of the One to whom we're praying." The power of prayer is not in the ones praying, but in the One listening.

Learning to pray
doesn't offer us a *less busy life;*
it offers us a **less busy heart.**

Paul Miller

In the midst of our busy lives, we can sometimes wonder whether we really have the time to pray. Won't prayer hinder our productivity? Won't prayer keep us from getting done all the things we need to do? When facing such questions, we would do well to consider that if we are too busy to pray, we are simply too busy! Martin Luther once lamented the busyness of his life but then exclaimed, "I have so much to do that I shall have to spend the first three hours in prayer!" Though he may have been speaking tongue-in-cheek, he meant to communicate something of the essential nature of prayer. He was too busy *not* to pray. And here Paul Miller speaks words of wisdom: "Learning to pray doesn't offer us a less busy life; it offers us a less busy heart." While praying will not check items off our too-long lists of things to do, it will quiet our hearts as we do them. It will enable us to submit ourselves, our responsibilities, and our to-dos to the one for whom we do them.

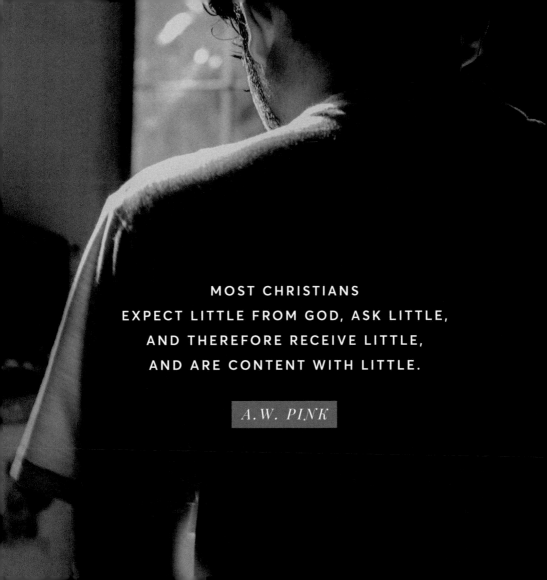

MOST CHRISTIANS
EXPECT LITTLE FROM GOD, ASK LITTLE,
AND THEREFORE RECEIVE LITTLE,
AND ARE CONTENT WITH LITTLE.

A.W. PINK

William Carey founded the modern missions movement on the conviction that we should expect great things from God and therefore attempt great things for God. And indeed, he and a generation of missionaries expected much, attempted much, and accomplished much to the glory of God. Perhaps Carey's words were in the back of A.W. Pink's mind when he pondered the tendency of Christians to expect too little from God. Though the Bible calls us to pray and though it promises that "the prayer of a righteous person has *great power* as it is working" (James 5:16), we can still have very modest expectations of what God will accomplish through our prayers. Because we expect little from God, we ask little. And because we ask little from God, we receive little. And because we grow so accustomed to receiving little from God, we grow content with little. We shape our prayers according to our expectations. If we would see God act in mighty ways, we must expect he will act in mighty ways and therefore pray for him to act in mighty ways.

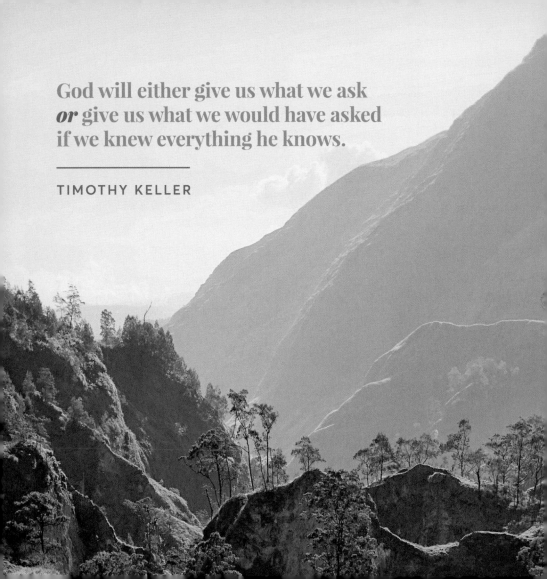

God will either give us what we ask *or* give us what we would have asked if we knew everything he knows.

TIMOTHY KELLER

When we pray to God and bring our petitions before him, and then say in earnest "thy will be done," how should we expect God to respond? Is asking God to overrule our will with his own admitting that he may actually bring us harm? Jesus answers when he asks rhetorically, "What father among you, if his son asks for a fish, will instead of a fish give him a serpent; or if he asks for an egg, will give him a scorpion?" (Luke 11:11-12). The confidence we have in our human fathers is the confidence we can have in our divine Father. "I tell you," he says, "ask, and it will be given to you; seek, and you will find; knock, and it will be opened to you" (verse 9). What will God give to those who ask? "God will either give us what we ask or give us what we would have asked if we knew everything he knows." To say "thy will be done" is to willingly and confidently admit that because of our limited knowledge and sinful desires, God must sometimes overrule us if he is ultimately to give us what is for our good and for his glory.

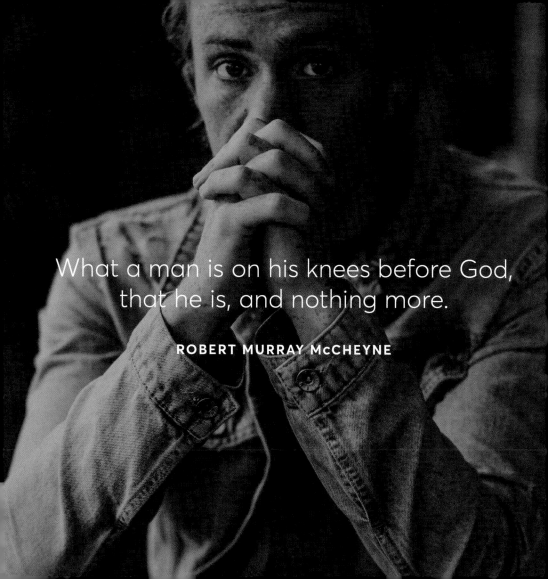

What a man is on his knees before God,
that he is, and nothing more.

ROBERT MURRAY McCHEYNE

Jesus, who knew what was in the heart of men, warned of the hypocrisy of those whose prayer life is only ever public. "When you pray," he said, "you must not be like the hypocrites. For they love to stand and pray in the synagogues and at the street corners, that they may be seen by others. Truly, I say to you, they have received their reward" (Matthew 6:5). The reward they longed for, they received—the recognition and acclamation of men. But we should desire something far higher and nobler than that. Hence, "when you pray, go into your room and shut the door and pray to your Father who is in secret. And your Father who sees in secret will reward you" (verse 6). When we desire the acclamation of God, when we desire his divine rewards, we gladly pray in secret, where no one but God can see us. We are content if our prayers are heard by God alone. We prove that we will forego the praise of men if only we can hear the "well done" of God. To be on our knees alone before God proves who and what we really are. It proves whom we really serve.

The angel fetched Peter out of prison, but it was prayer that fetched the angel.

THOMAS WATSON

We would not pray if we did not have confidence that God answers prayer. And indeed, his Word promises that he does. "This is the confidence that we have toward him, that if we ask anything according to his will he hears us. And if we know that he hears us in whatever we ask, we know that we have the requests that we have asked of him" (1 John 5:14-15). Because God answers prayer, and because God answers prayer according to his will, we ought to be diligent in looking for the ways he will answer. In Acts 12 we read of the early church praying that Peter would be rescued from his captivity. And as they prayed, God moved, sending an angel to save him. "The angel fetched Peter out of prison," says Thomas Watson, "but it was prayer that fetched the angel." Here, as in the history of the church and the stories of our own lives, God proves that it is his joy, his pleasure, to work through the prayers of his people. It is our duty to pray and then to watch to see *how* (not *if*) God will answer those prayers.

THE CHURCH
IS NOT MERELY A
ROSTER OF INDIVIDUALS
WHO PRAY PRIVATELY;
IT IS A CONGREGATION
THAT OUGHT TO PRAY
TOGETHER.

MEGAN HILL

Just as prayer is a crucial discipline for the individual believer, it is a crucial discipline for the assembled church. The Bible prescribes only a few elements for local church worship, but among them is prayer. While giving instructions to Pastor Timothy, Paul says, "I desire then that in every place the men should pray, lifting holy hands without anger or quarreling" (1 Timothy 2:8). Yet despite that insistence, perhaps no element of New Testament worship has fallen on harder times than congregational prayer. Though such prayer is commonly commanded and modeled in the pages of Scripture, it is often ignored. We neglect it at our peril, for God means to accomplish something through our corporate prayers. God means to bring unity to his people, for as prayer unites us in a common cause, it reminds us of our common Savior. It reminds us that "the church is not merely a roster of individuals who pray privately." It reminds us that we are members of one body, and that as such, we must pray to the one who is the head of the body, his church.

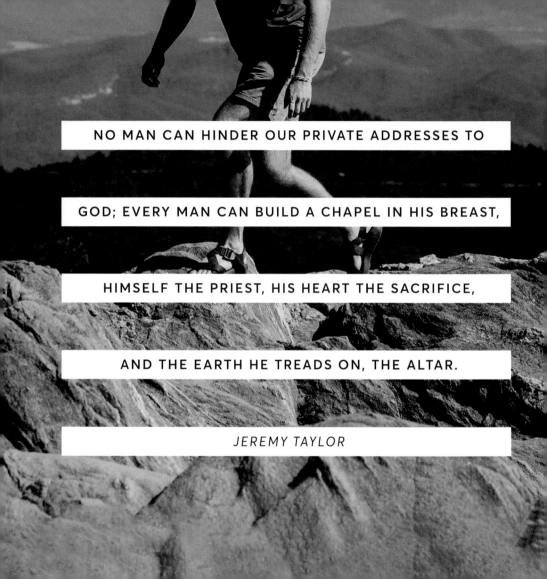

NO MAN CAN HINDER OUR PRIVATE ADDRESSES TO

GOD; EVERY MAN CAN BUILD A CHAPEL IN HIS BREAST,

HIMSELF THE PRIEST, HIS HEART THE SACRIFICE,

AND THE EARTH HE TREADS ON, THE ALTAR.

JEREMY TAYLOR

A woman from Samaria was once conversing with Jesus and puzzling over the answer to an age-old question: Where is the right place to worship? After all, the Jews and Samaritans worshipped in different places, each convinced theirs was the right and best place. But Jesus answered in a way neither Jew nor Samaritan would have expected: "Woman, believe me, the hour is coming when neither on this mountain nor in Jerusalem will you worship the Father.... The hour is coming, and is now here, when the true worshipers will worship the Father in spirit and truth" (John 4:21,23). And just as there is no right place to worship, there is no right place to pray, and just as there is no wrong place to worship, there is no wrong place to pray. No place is holier than any other. No matter where we are, no matter our circumstances, no one can keep us from praying, for as Jeremy Taylor says, "Every man can build a chapel in his breast, himself the priest, his heart the sacrifice, and the earth he treads on, the altar." Wherever we are, we have whatever we need.

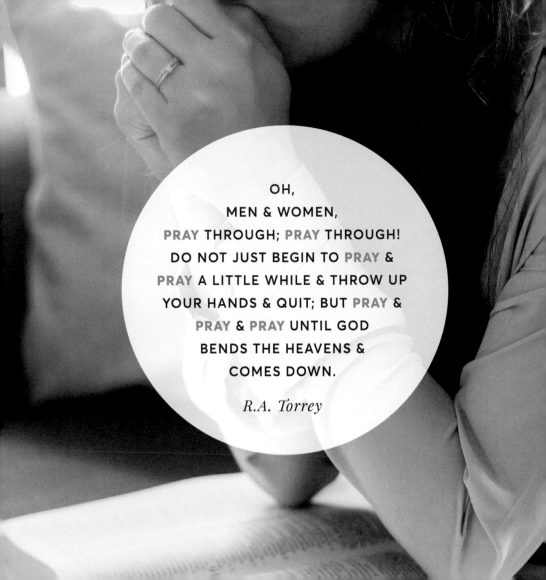

OH,
MEN & WOMEN,
PRAY THROUGH; PRAY THROUGH!
DO NOT JUST BEGIN TO PRAY &
PRAY A LITTLE WHILE & THROW UP
YOUR HANDS & QUIT; BUT PRAY &
PRAY & PRAY UNTIL GOD
BENDS THE HEAVENS &
COMES DOWN.

R.A. Torrey

When Jesus was facing the final hours of his life, he had no higher priority than prayer. He called upon his closest friends to join him that together they could cry out to the Father. But it was late at night and their eyes were heavy, and they soon fell asleep. Instead of praying with persistence, they gave up at the very first obstacle they encountered—the obstacle of their own physical weakness. And in their own way they represent all of us in our proneness to pray for a while and then to throw our hands up and quit. We begin with great earnestness and great conviction but then abandon our task at the first obstacle and the first moment it becomes difficult. And it is here that R.A. Torrey addresses our apathy, our lack of determination, our lack of persistence. "You do not have, because you do not ask," warns James (James 4:2). "Pray through; pray through!" cries Torrey. Don't allow obstacles to trip you up or cause you to give up. Rather, "Pray and pray and pray until God bends the heavens and comes down."

IF SINNERS BE DAMNED, AT LEAST

*let them leap
to Hell over
our bodies.*

IF THEY WILL PERISH, LET THEM PERISH
WITH OUR ARMS ABOUT THEIR KNEES.
LET NO ONE GO THERE UNWARNED
AND UNPRAYED FOR.

C.H. SPURGEON

One of the most sacred and most important of our tasks in prayer is to intercede on behalf of the lost. We know that every one of our friends and neighbors and family members needs to hear the good news of the gospel and repent and believe. We know that God is the Good Shepherd, who makes it his purpose to seek out and save the lost. We know that God hears the prayers of his people. And so of course we can and we should and we must pray that God would save them! We must pray that God would show them their lostness and show them the way to be found. We must pray that he would generate opportunities for us to share the gospel and that we would be obedient in accepting those opportunities and making the most of them, for it may be God's good pleasure not only to save them, but to use us as his instruments to do so. May Spurgeon's compassion for the lost and his passion for evangelizing them be reflected in all of us. "If sinners be damned, at least let them leap to Hell over our bodies. If they will perish, let them perish with our arms about their knees. Let no one go there unwarned and unprayed for."

Pray *when you feel* like it.
Pray *when you don't feel* like it.
Pray *until you feel* like it.

H.B. Charles Jr

It is wise to set aside a time and place to pray—to build the habit and to then maintain it. But creating the habit may not always create the desire. There will inevitably be occasions—sometimes a single day or sometimes a stretch of weeks—when we will not feel like praying. Our desires will be at war with our convictions. What are we to do when we know that God has called us to pray but we don't want to pray? H.B. Charles speaks to this situation when he says we are to pray when we feel like it *and* when we don't feel like it. This is precisely why we discipline ourselves to create habits, for our habits can help us do the right thing even when we don't particularly want to. But as we do the right thing anyway, we often find that our desires come into alignment with our convictions. It is often by our obedience that God addresses our desires. We pray when we don't feel like it so we will begin to feel like it!

*No time is so well spent in every day
as that which we spend upon our knees.*

J.C. RYLE

Each of us has many responsibilities. Each of us has goals we must accomplish, tasks we must perform, jobs we must complete, relationships we must nurture. We often find ourselves pulled this way and that, spread too thin across too many competing duties. And with so much to do, we can easily begin to wonder whether prayer is an appropriate use of scarce time. Wouldn't it be better to give my attention to something that would let me cross something off my to-do list? To even ask the question is to show that we haven't yet understood the unique importance of prayer. We haven't yet come to believe, as Ryle says, that "no time is so well spent in every day as that which we spend upon our knees." Yet Ryle meant it not just as a statement but as an exhortation, adding, "Let us be sure that no time is so well-spent in every day, as that which we spend upon our knees!" Let's be certain that our lives display the priority of prayer, the priority of speaking to our good and gracious Father who loves to hear from his children.

Our prayers run along one road,
and God's answers by another,

AND BY AND BY
THEY MEET.

God answers all true prayer,
either in kind or in kindness.

ADONIRAM JUDSON

God's knowledge of the present and future is as precise and exhaustive as his knowledge of the past. "I am God," he says, "and there is no other; I am God, and there is none like me, *declaring the end from the beginning* and *from ancient times things not yet done*, saying, 'My counsel shall stand, and I will accomplish all my purpose'" (Isaiah 46:9-10). Because we pray to a God who knows the future, we pray to a God who has already set aspects of that future into motion. We pray to a God who is already moving, already acting, already directing. As Adoniram Judson expresses here, it is like our prayers are running along one road while God's answers are running along another, and at some point they will meet, whether just a few steps farther on or far off in the distance. And when they do at last meet, we can be confident that we will receive either what we have asked (in kind) or what God has deemed even better (in kindness). Either way, we will receive what will best accomplish God's wonderful purposes for his people and his world.

God speaks to us through his Word, and we speak to him in prayer. These are means of grace that can be carried out in public or private. In fact, they are practices that are best carried out in both public *and* private—to read the Word on our own and with others, to pray privately and publicly. But there are means of grace that are essentially public, for we do not only read and listen, we also belong. We belong to God's community, his church. Our pursuit of God is not only a private pursuit but also a communal pursuit in which we join together with others.

Through the local church we read the Bible and pray together, but we do more than that—we also worship, we also fellowship, we also preach, we also participate in the ordinances (or sacraments, if you prefer). As we come to this final section of the book, we turn to quotes that focus on the joy of belonging to God's family, God's church.

The visible church is where you will find *Christ's kingdom* on earth, and to disregard *the kingdom* is to disregard *its King.*

— *Michael Horton*

After Jesus died and was resurrected, and immediately before he ascended to heaven, he told his disciples, "All authority in heaven and on earth has been given to me" (Matthew 28:18). Jesus is King and this world is his kingdom, given to him by the Father as a reward to the One who conquered death and the dominion of Satan. "He put all things under his feet and gave him as head over all things to the church, which is his body, the fullness of him who fills all in all" (Ephesians 1:22-23). Though Jesus is King, we can sometimes find ourselves looking at the kingdoms of mankind and despairing, for we see such evidence of rebellion and depravity. But where we see the outposts of Christ's kingdom, the clearest evidence of his victory, is in the local church. It is here, in the church, that we see visible evidence of Christ's victory. It is here we see the citizens of his kingdom living for the glory of their King. It is from here that we see the kingdom spread slowly but inexorably to the far corners of the earth and toward the great day when Christ will return.

Once you choose Christ,
you must choose His people, too.
—— *It's a package deal.* ——
Choose the Father & the Son & you
have to choose the whole family.

JONATHAN LEEMAN

Christ's kingdom is made manifest in the local church, for it is here that people join to bow the knee together to King Jesus, willingly pledging their loyalty to him. This pledge of loyalty creates a vertical relationship between the Christian and Christ, but it also creates a horizontal relationship between believers. John Wesley said rightly that "the Bible knows nothing of solitary religion."[6] Rather, the Bible calls us into fellowship with one another. In fact, it tells us that when we come to Christ, we become more than citizens of the same kingdom; we become brothers and sisters of the same family. "You are no longer strangers and aliens, but you are fellow citizens with the saints and *members of the household of God*" (Ephesians 2:19). When we choose Christ, we choose God as our Father and Christ as our King. But we do more than that, because as Jonathan Leeman says, "It's a package deal. Choose the Father and the Son and you have to choose the whole family." When you come to Christ, you enter into his family. As you gain a Savior, you necessarily also gain brothers and sisters.

If a person doesn't love the church, they don't love Jesus.

Voddie Baucham

God calls us to difficult things. He calls us not only to be part of a church but even to love the people of the church. We may find it easy enough to love a building or an institution or a particular form of worship. But people? That can be a much greater challenge because people are sinful, people are messy, people are needy. Yet our love for people cannot be separated from our love from God, for "if anyone says, 'I love God,' and hates his brother, he is a liar; for he who does not love his brother whom he has seen cannot love God whom he has not seen. And this commandment we have from him: whoever loves God must also love his brother" (1 John 4:20-21). Or as Voddie Baucham expresses it, if we don't love the church, we don't actually love Jesus. If we truly love Jesus, we will love the body of Jesus, the people of Jesus, the church of Jesus. Sinclair Ferguson says much the same thing in a slightly different way: "If Christ is not ashamed to indwell them I will not be slow to embrace them."[7] Who are we to reject the ones that Christ has accepted?

A CHURCH IS NOT A GROUP
OF FRIENDS YOU'VE PICKED,

IT'S A GROUP OF BROTHERS & SISTERS
GOD HAS PICKED FOR YOU.

Michael Horton

Though every child at times wishes it were otherwise, we do not get to choose our brothers and sisters. Rather, through the miracle of conception, God chooses who will join our families. And what is true of our birth families is in many ways true of our church families because both are involuntary communities. There are places in life where we choose to join together around a common cause or shared interest, and we can consider these voluntary communities since those who run the group have the right to welcome or to refuse anyone according to certain criteria. But church is involuntary in the sense that we do not choose whom God will lead to the church. This is by his design, for where we might attempt to custom-craft a church that looks perfect to our eyes, God has a higher purpose in mind. As Charles Drew says, "The church is supposed to be a sociological miracle—a demonstration that Jesus has died and risen to create a new humanity composed of all sorts of people."[8] Ultimately, we can rejoice that "a church is not a group of friends you've picked, it's a group of brothers and sisters God has picked for you."

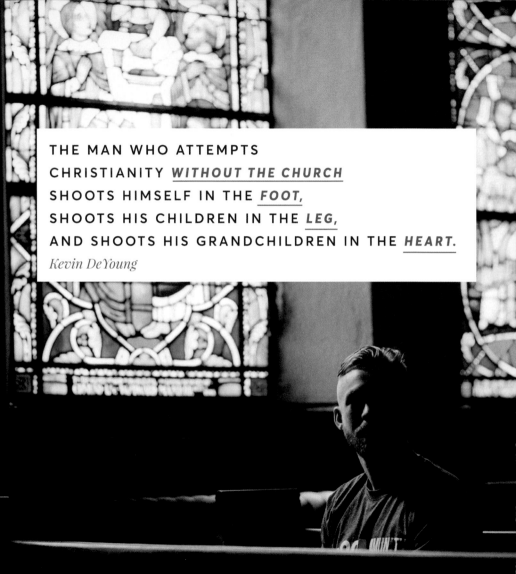

THE MAN WHO ATTEMPTS CHRISTIANITY *WITHOUT THE CHURCH* SHOOTS HIMSELF IN THE *FOOT*, SHOOTS HIS CHILDREN IN THE *LEG*, AND SHOOTS HIS GRANDCHILDREN IN THE *HEART*.

Kevin DeYoung

The Bible has much to say about creating legacies of faithfulness for our families. To parents falls the solemn responsibility of raising our children "in the discipline and instruction of the Lord" (Ephesians 6:4). God calls us not only to teach them the facts of the Christian faith but also to model before them the distinct character of a Christian. As we do so, our hope is reflected in a popular proverb: "Train up a child in the way he should go; even when he is old he will not depart from it" (Proverbs 22:6). Part of what we must model to our children is the centrality of the local church in the life and faith of the Christian. We must model what it is to do good to others, to persevere in local church fellowship, to respect church leadership, to participate in the means of grace. For just as the blessings of our obedience will flow out to them, so may the consequences of our disobedience. Kevin DeYoung offers a sober warning: "The man who attempts Christianity without the church shoots himself in the foot, shoots his children in the leg, and shoots his grandchildren in the heart."

THEY WHO WOULD GROW IN GRACE,

MUST LOVE THE HABITATION OF GOD'S HOUSE.

IT IS THOSE THAT ARE PLANTED IN THE COURTS OF THE

LORD WHO SHALL FLOURISH,

AND NOT THOSE THAT ARE OCCASIONALLY THERE.

JOHN
ANGELL
JAMES

Psalm 92 commends those who do not merely go through the outward motions of religion, but who genuinely and from the heart love to praise and honor God. "The righteous flourish like the palm tree and grow like a cedar in Lebanon. They are planted in the house of the LORD; they flourish in the courts of our God" (Psalm 92:12-13). These faithful ones are compared to a mighty and unshakeable tree that has been planted within the courts of the Old Testament temple. These believers are rooted in the place of worship and the forms of worship that God had established for them. It is not surprising, then, that "they still bear fruit in old age; they are ever full of sap and green" (verse 14). John Angell James picks up on that metaphor when he says that if we wish to grow in grace, we must love the context in which God has called us to worship—the local church. And if we wish to flourish there, we must make a firm commitment, not an occasional visit. We must be as grounded in the local church as that tree was in the courts of the temple.

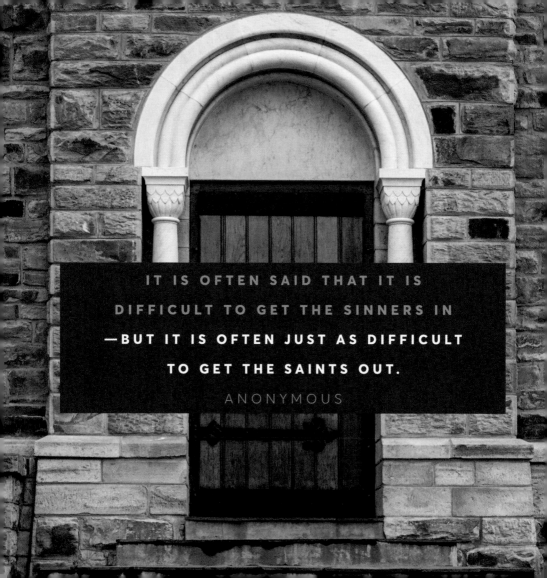

IT IS OFTEN SAID THAT IT IS DIFFICULT TO GET THE SINNERS IN —BUT IT IS OFTEN JUST AS DIFFICULT TO GET THE SAINTS OUT.

ANONYMOUS

Though the local church is a community of Christians and exists primarily for the benefit of Christians, it is also a community that gladly welcomes as guests those who are not yet believers. Many churches rightly put a lot of effort into inviting friends, neighbors, and family members to this place where they can hear the gospel preached and see Christian community in action. Yet we often face this challenge, this tragedy: Even as we put effort into calling sinners to come into Christ's kingdom, we have to put equal effort into calling the saved to come out to church. As one wag has said, "It takes ninety gallons of water to baptize a Christian and only nine drops of rain to keep him at home!" The Bible warns against "neglecting to meet together, as is the habit of some," but instead advocates corporately "encouraging one another, and all the more as you see the Day drawing near" (Hebrews 10:25). Each of us has needs that can be filled only by other believers, and each of us has gifts that are meant to serve other believers. It is our joy and our duty to exercise them each and every week.

I have no doubt that
the Lord can see more fault
in His church than I can;
& I have equal confidence that
He sees no fault at all.

CHARLES SPURGEON

It has often been said that church would be perfect if it weren't for all the people! And it is true that wherever there are people, there will be struggles and there will be conflicts. It's noteworthy that among Jesus's first and most explicit instructions about the local church are the ones that pertain to the resolution of interpersonal conflict (Matthew 18:15-20). Yet it's equally true that the unity of Christ's people is meant to be a unique mark of the church and one that will be attractive to others. Jesus said, "Just as I have loved you, you also are to love one another. By this all people will know that you are my disciples, if you have love for one another" (John 13:34-35). We are prone to find fault in the local church and especially in the other members of the local church. We can allow the sins and imperfections of others to drive us away from fellowship. But perhaps, like Spurgeon, we should take our inspiration from Jesus. Though his all-seeing eye and all-knowing mind spots every imperfection, he still draws near instead of running away.

AS YOU PASS
THROUGH THE VALLEY OF
THE SHADOW OF DEATH, AND THE
SHEPHERD COMFORTS YOU WITH
HIS STAFF, YOU WILL DISCOVER
THAT HE HAS FASHIONED HIS
PEOPLE TO ACT AS HIS
ROD OF RESCUE.

David Mathis

It is for good reason that so many Christians commit Psalm 23 to memory, for as it tells of the love of the Shepherd for his sheep, and as it describes the tender protection of his flock, it assures us that God is leading and guiding us through the dark valleys of our lives. "Even though I walk through the valley of the shadow of death, I will fear no evil, for you are with me; your rod and your staff, they comfort me" (Psalm 23:4). The rod and the staff were the instruments a shepherd would use to guard and to protect, to drive wolves away and to draw sheep close. Each of us passes through dark valleys of pain and suffering and other forms of difficulty, and what Mathis wants us to consider is that often the Shepherd's means of protection is not a wooden rod or staff, but our fellow sheep, our brothers and sisters in Christ. For as James says, "My brothers, if anyone among you wanders from the truth and someone brings him back, let him know that whoever brings back a sinner from his wandering will save his soul from death and will cover a multitude of sins" (James 5:19-20).

As secret worship is

BETTER

the more secret it is,

so public worship is

BETTER

the more public it is.

MATTHEW HENRY

It is good to worship God in secret, where no one can see us except the Lord. In fact, the most effective secret worship is the most secret of secret worship, those times when we are truly alone with the Lord. But it is also good and necessary to worship God in public, for God has things to accomplish in our worship that can only be completed when we worship with other believers. That being the case, the most effective public worship is the most public of public worship. Donald Whitney says, "There's an element of worship and Christianity that cannot be experienced in private worship or by watching worship. There are some graces and blessings that God gives only in 'meeting together' with other believers."[9] What are these graces? They are the preaching of the Word, the administration of the sacraments (or ordinances, if you prefer), and the pursuit of Christian fellowship. These are means of grace that are experienced in an exclusive way or in a special way through the local church. They are a necessarily public component of our Christian lives in which we live in view of not only the Father but also our brothers and sisters.

CORPORATE WORSHIP IS A REGULAR
GRACIOUS REMINDER THAT IT'S NOT ABOUT YOU.
YOU'VE BEEN BORN INTO A LIFE THAT
IS A CELEBRATION OF ANOTHER.

PAUL DAVID TRIPP

Every Christian knows it is both our duty and our delight to gather with God's people on each Lord's Day. But we may have less clarity on why we do this. Why is it so important that we gather specifically to *worship*? The answer goes all the way back to the Garden of Eden and to mankind's catastrophic fall into sin. When we turned away from God, we turned toward ourselves. The natural inclination of our hearts was no longer outward to God, but inward toward ourselves (2 Timothy 3:2). Our deepest loyalty, and therefore our most heartfelt worship, was directed to ourselves rather than to our Creator. But then God saved us, and in saving us he restored our desire and our ability to put him first in our hearts, in our lives, and in our worship. Now every week we gather together with our Christian brothers and sisters to remind ourselves and one another that it's not about us! As we begin a new week, we proclaim that we've been born again into a whole new life, a whole new kind of life, that is oriented toward bringing glory to God.

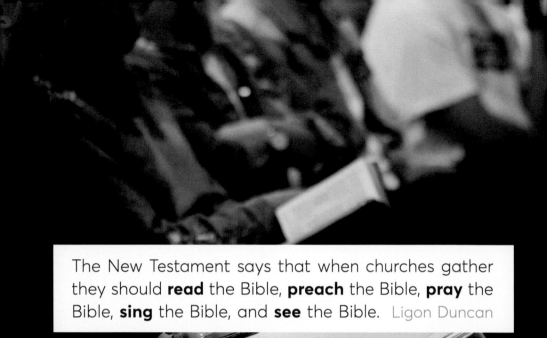

The New Testament says that when churches gather they should **read** the Bible, **preach** the Bible, **pray** the Bible, **sing** the Bible, and **see** the Bible. Ligon Duncan

Many of us live in contexts and cultures in which there is fierce competition among churches, each advertising itself as more interesting, more appealing, more entertaining than the others. It sometimes seems that no gimmick is too crass and no strategy too absurd for these churches as they attempt to one-up the others and fill their pews. Yet the Bible has little time for such novel and inventive strategies, for God tells us how we are to worship him. He makes it clear that our worship is to be centered around his Word so that every part of our public worship is drenched in the Bible. A worship service without the Bible is, quite simply, not a worship service at all! As we gather to worship, then, we are to read the Bible so God can speak to us. We are to preach the Bible so a preacher can exposit that Word and apply it to us. We are to pray the words of the Bible and to ask God to drive it home in our hearts and lives. We are to sing songs that declare the great doctrines of the Bible. And we are to "see" the Bible as its truths are pictured in baptism and the Lord's Supper. We are people who are utterly dependent upon the Word and who therefore, week by week, gather around the Word.

For all the noise ministers make about
the centrality of the Bible in the church,
the public reading of Scripture in many places
does not *support that conviction.*

FRED CRADDOCK

Every new Christian is told how important it is to develop the habit of daily Bible reading, and rightly so. But strangely, this commitment to reading the Bible is not as often extended to the worship services of the local church. The public reading of Scripture seems to have been displaced in a great many local churches, perhaps because it is deemed boring or perhaps because the pastor is content to focus on just a handful of verses during a sermon. Yet the apostle Paul specifically told young Pastor Timothy, "Devote yourself to the public reading of Scripture" (1 Timothy 4:13). We may see Bible reading as a lesser element in our corporate worship, but God sees it as essential. For that reason we must be as eager to hear the Scripture as to hear the sermon, and we must be as expectant that God will speak to us through the Word as through the message. Rightly do many churches preface their Bible reading with words like, "Listen as I read God's holy Word." May our attitude be like Samuel's: "Speak, for your servant hears" (1 Samuel 3:10).

HOLY WRIT IS TO BE KEPT NOT UNDER A BUSHEL,
but under men's noses.
ITS MESSAGE IS TO BE HELD FORTH
AS DILIGENTLY AS IT IS HELD FAST.

J.I. Packer

Many cold and lifeless churches testify to the fact that the mere presence of the Bible is no guarantee of spiritual life and vigor. Many churches have a Bible tucked neatly into every pew but teach a message radically at odds with the words of that very Book. The task of the church is not merely to provide a physical copy of the Bible, but to carefully teach the contents of the Bible. If "Holy Writ is to be kept not under a bushel," as Packer says, then surely it's not to be kept in the pew. Rather, it is to be kept under the noses of the congregation— to be opened and read. The Bible is not to be held fast as some kind of Christian artifact, but held forth as the words of life. Again, it must be opened and it must be read! It must be read aloud in the presence of the church, where the whole congregation can hear it together and respond to it together! Every week every Christian can anticipate hearing the voice of God as he speaks through the voice of the person who opens that sacred Book and says, "Listen as I read God's holy Word." Rightly do God's people respond to that reading with a hearty "Amen!"

WHERE THE AUTHENTIC

PREACHING OF THE WORD TAKES PLACE,

the church is there.

AND WHERE THAT IS ABSENT,

there is no church.

NO MATTER HOW HIGH THE STEEPLE,

NO MATTER HOW LARGE THE BUDGET,

NO MATTER HOW IMPRESSIVE THE MINISTRY,

it is something else.

Albert Mohler

A well-known pastor was once asked whether he was offended that a new church near his had taken on the same name. "Are you offended that they are also calling themselves Grace Church?" "No," he replied. "I'm not bothered that they are calling themselves 'Grace.' I'm bothered that they are calling themselves a church!" Christians have long had to determine what marks a true church in contrast to a false church. Looking to the New Testament, they've long determined that it is not the name, the building, the budget, or the ministries that determine whether a particular group of people forms a church. Rather, it is the presence of preaching—true preaching that proclaims the precious truths of God's Word. Albert Mohler says it plainly: "Where the authentic preaching of the Word takes place, the church is there. And where that is absent, there is no church." When Christians gather to worship, there is no means of grace more prominent or more powerful than the preaching of God's holy Word.

*Preaching is the miracle of God communicating Himself
to a fallen world through the words of a fallen man.*

BRIAN EDWARDS

Over the course of our Christian lives we hear hundreds or even thousands of sermons. Perhaps through the sheer repetition we are prone to forget what makes preaching so special, so unique. At the heart of preaching is the wonder—what Brian Edwards calls the miracle—of God communicating to us through other human beings. Preachers of no particular eloquence plainly preach a straightforward message whose content seems simplistic and even offensive to many. Yet that simple preaching of that simple message brings life from death, for "the foolishness of God is wiser than men, and the weakness of God is stronger than men" (1 Corinthians 1:25). God means to upend both the methods and the messages of the world. In contrast to a message that inevitably makes man look great, God brings a message that makes man look small. In contrast to methods that rely on persuasive speaking or rhetorical gimmicks, God uses the simplest of men who speak the plainest of words. Each Sunday he communicates to fallen men through fallen men to save his people and to sanctify them.

Prayer can no more be divorced from worship than life can be divorced from breathing.

Robert Kendall

When we think of worship, our thoughts almost always gravitate to singing—the two have become inseparable and almost synonymous in our minds and in our church services. Yet singing is actually just one component of worship. We worship when we sing, but we also worship when we read Scripture, when we listen to a sermon, when we celebrate the Lord's Supper, when we fellowship together. And of course if all that is true, then we also worship when we pray. In fact, prayer is integral to our worship, for if we are to worship God in Spirit and in truth, we must have God's help, which is exactly why a prayer of invocation is a traditional element of a service. It is through prayer that we express our dependence upon God and through prayer that we call upon him—invoke him—to be present with us and to enable us to worship him in ways that are pleasing to him. Through prayer we acknowledge that without God's help our best worship will be nothing but a passionate, heartfelt sin. We cannot worship without praying any more than we can live without breathing.

*The pastor who is
not _praying is playing;_
the people who are not
praying are straying.*

Leonard Ravenhill

Christians have long compared prayer to a thermometer that measures spiritual heat. When we grow complacent in our relationship with the Lord, that thermometer almost invariably registers cool, for in such times we pray seldom and we pray without fervor. What is true of us individually is true of us congregationally. We need to be constantly on guard against encroaching apathy, and such spiritual malaise often manifests itself first in prayerlessness. The pastor who is not praying *for* his congregation and *with* his congregation may be doing little more than playing pastor, for he is neglecting one of his most solemn duties. The congregation that is not praying on their own and when assembled may well already be straying from the will of the Lord, for they are neglecting to adequately care for one another (James 5:16). Congregational prayer is a crucial component of our worship and a key measure of our spiritual health. In the absence of prayer is the presence of spiritual sickness.

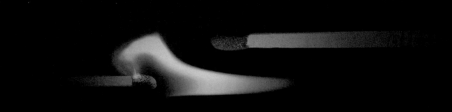

**SOME PEOPLE'S PRAYERS NEED
TO BE CUT OFF AT BOTH ENDS
& SET ON FIRE IN THE MIDDLE.**

D.L. Moody

Sometimes humor accomplishes what soberness cannot, as this quote demonstrates. We have all had to endure prayers that were a little too long (or perhaps a lot too long) or that could have used a little more preparation (or perhaps a lot more preparation). We ought to understand public prayer as a responsibility to take seriously and a privilege to steward faithfully. No preacher would show up on Sunday morning without having first prepared a sermon, but many pray-ers show up on Sunday morning without having given a thought to how they will lead others in speaking to the Lord. These tend to be the prayers that, to echo Moody, need to have a little trimmed from the beginning, a little more trimmed from the end, and a whole lot more heart and soul inserted into the middle. Spurgeon explains well that the most important preparation is preparation of the heart "which consists in the solemn consideration beforehand of the importance of prayer, meditation upon the needs of men's souls, and a remembrance of the promises we are to plead; and thus coming before the Lord with a petition written upon the fleshly tables of the heart."[10] This is prayer that honors God and serves the church.

A CHURCH'S SONGS ARE NOT A
MERE PREAMBLE TO THE SERMON.
SINGING IS NOT FILLER TIME
TO WARM UP A CONGREGATION.
SINGING IS A HOLY PRACTICE.
WE SING BECAUSE GOD HAS
COMMANDED US, AND OUR SONGS SHOULD
FILL OUR HEARTS WITH DELIGHT.

MATT BOSWELL

While it may be rare to find a church that dedicates a substantial portion of the service to prayers and Scripture reading, it would be rare to find a church that fails to dedicate a substantial portion of the service to singing. Christians love to sing, and we have always regarded it as an essential component of our worship. In Paul's letter to the Colossians he says, "Let the word of Christ dwell in you richly, teaching and admonishing one another in all wisdom, singing psalms and hymns and spiritual songs, with thankfulness in your hearts to God" (3:16). Singing is to be corporate so that the whole congregation joins their voices together as one. And that singing is meant to be both horizontal—a means to encourage and strengthen one another—and vertical—a means to express our thanks and praise to God. This being the case, our songs must be meaty, for they need to teach and admonish our brothers and sisters while also communicating gratitude to the Lord. We sing *from* the Word, *for* one another, and *to* the Lord.

Your voice may not be of professional standard,
but it is of confessional standard.

Keith Getty

God commands us to sing. Yet while some of God's people are gifted singers, the plain fact is that others are not. In any congregation it's likely that some have near-perfect pitch while others are functionally tone-deaf. Those who struggle to sing may be self-conscious, tempted to stay quiet or to do no more than mumble along. Should they? Not at all, for singing is a matter of the heart before it is a matter of pitch or tone. In Ephesians 5:18-19 Paul writes, "Be filled with the Spirit, addressing one another in psalms and hymns and spiritual songs, singing and making melody to the Lord *with your heart*." What matters far more than the sound that comes out of the mouth is the posture of the heart. There is more beauty in an off-pitch voice that is the outpouring of a submissive heart than in a perfectly pitched voice that is the outpouring of a rebellious heart. Though few Christians have voices that are truly professional, every Christian has a voice that can be confessional—that confesses and publicly professes the great truths of the Christian faith. Jonathan Leeman says rightly that "the most beautiful instrument in any Christian service is the sound of the congregation singing."[11]

The ordinances are the dramatic presentations of the gospel. They are the moving pictures that represent the spiritual realities of the gospel, written & directed by Jesus himself.

MARK DEVER

As we gather on Sundays, we preach the Bible, read the Bible, pray the Bible, and sing the Bible. But that is not all, for we also "see" the Bible. God has given us two ordinances (or sacraments, if you prefer) that present the gospel in a very different way. Instead of hearing it or speaking it, we see it. We see it demonstrated through baptism and the Lord's Supper. These too are means of God's grace, and Ligon Duncan explains it in this way: "In the reading and preaching of the Word, God addresses our mind and conscience through the hearing. In the sacraments, he uniquely addresses our mind and conscience through the other senses."[12] In baptism and the Lord's Supper, God blesses and strengthens us as we see these moving pictures and as we touch, taste, and smell water, bread, and wine. These are the little plays, the little demonstrations, Christ himself has given us through which we experience his blessings, his sanctifying and sustaining grace.

IF YOU WANT TO
IDENTIFY YOURSELF WITH
CHRIST'S PEOPLE AND EXPECT
THEM TO IDENTIFY WITH YOU,
YOU NEED TO FIRST IDENTIFY
YOURSELF WITH CHRIST,
WHICH IS THE PURPOSE
OF BAPTISM.

JONATHAN LEEMAN

Each of the ordinances has a distinct purpose and a distinct role in the life of the Christian. Baptism is an initiatory rite, a means by which a person publicly identifies with Christ Jesus—an occasion of joy and blessing not only for the person being baptized but for the entire church. This act pictures something, but it also accomplishes something. In the washing with water in the name of the Father, Son, and Holy Spirit, we see a picture of being cleansed from sin, of being raised from death to life, and of passing safely through the waters of judgment. And that same washing with water in the name of the Tri-une God is spiritually significant in that it seals our adoption and our entrance into the family of God. Through this sign and seal we come to be identified with Christ and with his people. Through it we are initiated into his family, into his church. After we are baptized, it is right and good for other Christians to acknowledge what it has signi-fied and sealed—we are brothers and sisters of a common Father.

The Lord's Supper is a badge of belonging just as much as baptism is. **Baptism is the front door of the house, & the Lord's Supper is the family meal.**

Bobby Jamieson

Baptism is a kind of front door to the local church, the God-ordained means through which a person identifies with Jesus Christ and formally comes to belong to Christ's body, the church. Baptism is the church's sign that this person is one of us, a brother or sister in the Lord, who has now been welcomed into the house through the front door. And just like baptism proves that a person belongs, so too does the Lord's Supper. Bobby Jamieson says that if baptism can be understood as the front door of the house, then the Lord's Supper can be understood as the family meal for all the members of the house. The family is identified by walking through the front door, and the family then celebrates and signifies their unity by enjoying a meal together. Through this meal, God nourishes and strengthens us as individuals while also drawing us together as a family. As Christ says "Take, eat; this is my body" and "Drink of it, all of you, for this is my blood of the covenant" (Matthew 26:26-28), he feeds our faith, he stirs our hearts, he causes us to grow in love, grace, and obedience.

IT IS
TRUE THAT
THE LORD'S SUPPER
IS ONLY FOR SINNERS.
BUT WITHIN THAT GROUP,
IT IS ONLY FOR
REPENTANT
SINNERS.

Mark Dever

Sometimes there is encouragement embedded in a warning, and that is exactly the case with these words from Mark Dever. Many Christians feel they are too unholy or too sinful to participate in the Lord's Supper. They come to the table downcast, convinced that their sin makes them unworthy. They may refuse to participate at all. But the reality is that being a sinner and having an awareness of that sin is not a hindrance to the Lord's Supper, but a prerequisite. It is sinners who are invited to the table because it is sinners who need the table. "Those who are well have no need of a physician, but those who are sick. I came not to call the righteous, but sinners" (Mark 2:17). The Savior who calls sinners to himself, calls sinners to his table. Yet as Dever points out, it is a particular kind of sinner—a repentant sinner. We dare not come if we are reveling in our sin, enjoying it, refusing to turn from it. But we dare not refuse to come if we hate our sin, if we are living lives of repentance, if we know our need of the Savior, who says, "This is my body, which is given for you. Do this in remembrance of me" (Luke 22:19).

CONCLUSION

We have marveled at the reality that God invites us into relationship with himself—we can know God! We have established the importance of being disciplined in our relationship with God by building habits through which we will continue to pursue and prioritize the means of grace. We have seen the beauty of hearing from God through his Word; we have considered the wonder that we can speak to God, knowing he hears, knowing he listens; we have expressed gratitude for the local church through which we join with other Christians to read the Bible, preach the Bible, pray the Bible, sing the Bible, and see the Bible. All that remains, then, is to offer some concluding reflections that offer us both warnings and encouragement.

Neither be idle in the means,
NOR MAKE AN IDOL OF THE MEANS.

William Secker

As we draw to the end of this series of quotes and reflections, it seems fitting that we remind ourselves of the power and purpose of these disciplines of hearing from God, speaking to God, and belonging to God. As Christians through the centuries have pondered these means of grace, these key habits of the Christian life, they have always felt the need to address two equal and opposite temptations. The first temptation is to neglect the means of grace, and the second is to idolize the means of grace. Some grow weary of the repetition and sheer ordinariness of these means. They find themselves longing for something new, something extraordinary, and are tempted to neglect them. But then others, while practicing these habits day by day and week by week, can begin to find that their spiritual confidence is no longer in Christ but in these habits. They have essentially replaced their faith in Christ with faith in Christ's means of grace. Some become idle in their use of the ordinary means, while others make these ordinary means into an idol. This is why John Trapp warns that "means must be neither trusted nor neglected."[13] With your heart fixed firmly in Christ, with your faith secure in him, you can practice these means not to gain his favor, but to enjoy it.

When a Christian
shuns fellowship
with other Christians,
the devil smiles.
When he stops
studying the Bible,
the devil laughs.
When he stops praying,
the devil shouts for joy.

CORRIE TEN BOOM

Jesus triumphed over Satan at the cross, and though Satan's doom is sure, he remains dangerous even in his death throes. He is active in our lives, still the tempter, still the adversary of God and his people. "Be sober-minded; be watchful," warns Peter. "Your adversary the devil prowls around like a roaring lion, seeking someone to devour" (1 Peter 5:8). If these means of grace are the habits through which we enjoy Christ, the habits through which we grow in knowledge and obedience, we should expect the devil to do all he can to keep us from them. He will do what he can to interfere or to influence us away from the Bible, away from prayer, and away from worship and fellowship. As we fall away from the company of our brothers and sisters, as we grow distant from the voice of God through his Word, as we grow lackadaisical in speaking to God through prayer, Satan smiles, he laughs, he shouts for joy. Our sorrow is his pleasure. But "resist the devil, and he will flee from you," says James (James 4:7). We must resist him, and we can resist him, for Satan has no authority over those who are in Christ.

When we are out of the way of duty,
we are in the way of temptation.

———————————————

MATTHEW HENRY

We do not often speak of duty today, but Christians traditionally understood the means of grace as duties, responsibilities of every believer toward God. And while these duties are the means through which God provides us with his grace, they are also the means through which God guards us against temptation. Christians who wish to overcome the inevitable temptations of the world, the flesh, and the devil must remain dutiful, alert, and disciplined. As we fall away from these habits, we should not be surprised when we face increased temptation and when we more easily succumb to these temptations. Charles Spurgeon once wrote, "Idle people tempt the devil to tempt them."[14] And indeed, the devil is most active when we are most idle—especially in the spiritual disciplines. Matthew Henry says, "When we are out of the way of duty, we are in the way of temptation." If that is true, so is the inverse: When we are in the way of duty, we are out of the way of temptation. This is not to say that when we take full advantage of the habits of grace we will face no temptation, but that when we do face temptation, we will readily avail ourselves of the means through which we can face it and triumph over it.

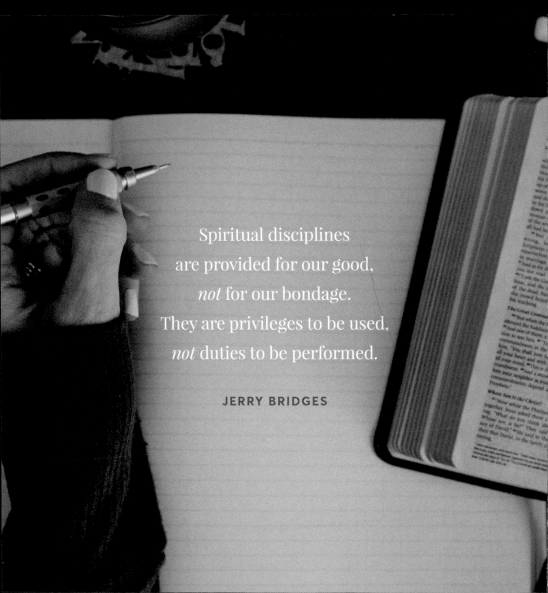

Spiritual disciplines
are provided for our good,
not for our bondage.
They are privileges to be used,
not duties to be performed.

JERRY BRIDGES

Matthew Henry says that "when we are out of the way of duty, we are in the way of temptation." Yet Jerry Bridges warns that the spiritual disciplines are "privileges to be used, not duties to be performed." So are these duties or are they not? There is no contradiction here, for the key is in the word "performed." As we come to the end of this book, it seems fitting that we should be reminded once more of the temptation to misuse things—even things as good as the means of grace. Instead of understanding them as privileges given by God for our good and our joy, we are never far from mistaking them as obligations we merely carry out in a cold and unfeeling way. Instead of seeing them as habits that flow out of our salvation, we see them as obligations that merit our salvation. Instead of being freed by them, we become enslaved to them. Instead of enjoying them, we perform them. And so we need this reminder from Bridges that they are given for our good; they are privileges we are meant to enjoy, not duties we are meant to merely perform. They are not the means to the favor of God, but to the grace of God.

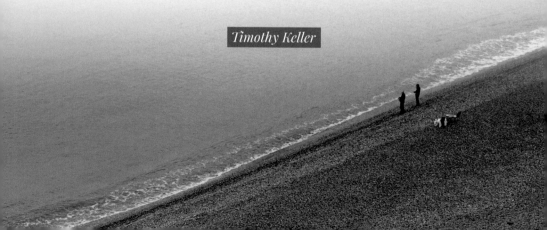

The gospel is this:

WE ARE MORE SINFUL AND FLAWED IN

OURSELVES THAN WE EVER DARED BELIEVE,

yet at the very same time

WE ARE MORE LOVED AND

ACCEPTED IN JESUS CHRIST THAN

WE EVER DARED HOPE.

Timothy Keller

We must end with the gospel, with the good news, the great news, the wondrous news, the sends-chills-up-my-spine news, the brings-tears-to-my-eyes news, the I-wouldn't-believe-it-if-God-hadn't-said-it news of what Jesus Christ has accomplished on our behalf. As we grow in our relationship to God, we will be faced ever more with the sorrowful reality of our own sinfulness. The closer we come to the Pacific Ocean, the more we realize its vastness and our own smallness; the closer we come to God, the more we understand his perfection and our sinfulness. As we come to a greater knowledge of both God and ourselves, we inevitably realize "we are more sinful and flawed in ourselves than we ever dared believe." Yet the news is not all bad. To the contrary, it's gloriously good, for "at the very same time we are more loved and accepted in Jesus Christ than we ever dared hope." This is the gospel in its glory—we are accepted, we are loved, we are Christ's.

ACKNOWLEDGMENTS

Together we would like to extend our gratitude to Harvest House Publishers (and Heather Green in particular) for taking an interest in this project and for the long commitment to it. And we would like to thank Andrew Wolgemuth and the rest of Wolgemuth & Associates for their guidance and assistance.

FROM TIM

My gratitude goes, as always, to my family for their love and support through yet another book project. And to Jules for teaming up with me on literally thousands of these SquareQuotes over the years.

FROM JULES

I am grateful to my coauthor Tim and for Andrew from Wolgemuth & Associates for relentlessly pursuing the vision of this project in its entirety. To my family for their generous love and loyalty. For the close friendships of those who have supported me throughout this tumultuous year in persistent prayer and encouragement. For challenging me to grow in my faith and to love God with my whole heart, soul, and mind every day. And to God, who sustains my every breath.

NOTES

1 John Piper, "Books Don't Change People, Paragraphs Do," Desiring God, July 16, 2013, https://www.desiringgod.org/articles/books-dont-change-people-paragraphs-do.

2 Visit http://squarequotes.church to see the thousands we've created so far.

3 John Calvin, *Calvin's Institutes*, ed. Donald McKaim (Louisville, KY: Westminster John Knox Press, 2000), 1.

4 Charles Spurgeon, "Satan Considering the Saints," sermon 623 in *The Complete Works of C.H. Spurgeon*, vol. 11, *Sermons 607-667* (Fort Collins, CO: Delmarva, 2013), point 2.

5 John Bunyon, *The Whole Works of That Eminent Servant of Christ...Mr. John Bunyan, in Six Volumes*, vol. 4 (London, UK: Alex. Hogg, 1784), 2124.

6 John Wesley, *The Heart of Wesley's Journal* (Peabody, MA: Hendrickson, 2008), 11.

7 Sinclair Ferguson, "Union with Christ: Life-Transforming Implications," sermon, Desiring God Conference for Pastors, Minneapolis, MN, February 4, 2014.

8 Charles Drew, *A Journey Worth Taking* (Phillipsburg, NJ: P&R, 2007).

9 Donald Whitney, *Spiritual Disciplines for the Christian Life* (Colorado Springs, CO: NavPress, 1997), 92.

10 Charles Spurgeon, *The Pastor in Prayer* (Edinburgh, UK: Banner of Truth Trust, 2004), 183.

11 Jonathan Leeman, *Reverberation: How God's Word Brings Light, Freedom, and Action to His People* (Chicago, IL: Moody, 2011).

12 Ligon Duncan, "What does biblically directed and informed public worship look like?" LigonDuncan.com, July 11, 2014, https://ligonduncan.com/what-does-biblically-directed-and-informed-public-worship-look-like/.

13 John Trapp, *A Commentary on the Old and New Testaments*, vol. 1 (London, England: Richard Dickinson, 1867), 106.

14 Charles Spurgeon, "Satan Considering the Saints," sermon 623 in *The Complete Works of C.H. Spurgeon*, vol. 11, *Sermons 607-667* (Fort Collins, CO: Delmarva, 2013), point 2.

SQUAREQUOTES CITATIONS

Page 8: J.I. Packer, *Knowing God* (Downer's Grove, IL: IVP Academic, 1993), location 446.

Page 10: C.S. Lewis, *Mere Christianity* (Harper Collins, 2001), 164-165.

Page 12: Cited in John Blanchard, *The Complete Gathered Gold* (Darlington, UK: Evangelical Press, 2006).

Page 14: Erwin Lutzer, "The Difference Between General and Special Revelations," Moody Church Media, https://www.moodymedia.org/articles/difference-between-general-and-special-revelation4s/.

Page 16: Thomas Brooks, *Paradise Opened*, first published in 1675, available online at https://www.monergism.com/thethreshold/sdg/brooks/Paradise_Opened_-_Thomas_Brooks.pdf.

Page 18: Sam Storms, *One Thing* (Fearn, UK: Christian Focus Publications, 2004), 87.

Page 20: Daryl Wingerd, "The Bible Is God's Special Revelation," Christian Communicators Worldwide, April 9, 2008, https://www.ccwtoday.org/2008/04/the-bible-is-gods-special-revelation/.

Page 22: Sam Stephens, "General Revelation," Association of Certified Biblical Counselors, November 29, 2018, https://biblicalcounseling.com/general-revelation/.

Page 24: Donald G. Bloesch, *A Theology of Word and Spirit* (Downers Grove, IL: InterVarsity Press, 1992), 20.

Page 26: Michael Lawrence, *Biblical Theology in the Life of the Church* (Weaton, IL: Crossway, 2010), 17. This is Lawrence's paraphrase of Horton's original quote: "God's speaking is acting, and this acting is not only descriptive and propositional; it is also creative and performative." Michael Horton, *People and Place: A Covenant of Ecclesiology* (Louisville, KY: John Knox Press, 2008) 40.

Page 30: Donald Whitney, *Spiritual Disciplines for the Christian Life* (Carol Stream, IL: Tyndale House, 1991), 243.

Page 32: David Mathis, *Habits of Grace* (Wheaton, IL: Crossway, 2016).

Page 34: John Piper, *Why I Love the Apostle Paul* (Wheaton, IL: Crossway, 2019), 136.

Page 36: A.W. Tozer, *The Pursuit of God*, first published in 1948, available online at http://www.gutenberg.org/ebooks/25141.

Page 38: Donald Whitney, *Spiritual Disciplines for the Christian Life* (Carol Stream, IL: Tyndale House, 1991), 17.

Page 40: J.C. Ryle, *Holiness*, first published in 1877, available online at https://www.monergism.com/holiness-ebook.

Page 42: Jerry Bridges, *Transforming Grace* (Colorado Springs, CO: NavPress, 1991), 128.

Page 44: David Mathis, *Habits of Grace* (Wheaton, IL: Crossway, 2016).

Page 46: Thomas Watson, "The Sixth Petition in the Lord's Prayer," in *The Lord's Prayer*, first published in 1692, available online at https://www.monergism.com/holiness-ebook.

Page 48: Jerry Bridges, *The Discipline of Grace* (Colorado Springs, CO: NavPress, 1994), 19. The original begins with the word "our."

Page 52: Thomas Guthrie, *The Way to Life: Sermons* (Edinburgh, UK: Adam and Charles Black, 1862), 91.

Page 54: Cited in Martin Manser, *The Westminster Collection of Christian Quotations* (Louisville, KY: Westminster John Knox Press, 2001), 21.

Page 56: Alistair Begg, *Preaching for God's Glory*, repackaged ed. (Wheaton, IL: Crossway, 2010), 46.

Page 58: Cited in John MacArthur, *How to Study the Bible* (Chicago, IL: Moody, 2009), 19.

Page 60: Nancy DeMoss Wolgemuth, *The Quiet Place: Daily Devotional Readings* (Chicago, IL: Moody, 2012), 24.

Page 62: Cited in Howard Books, *God's Help for Your Every Need: 101 Life-Changing Prayers* (New York, NY: Howard Books, 2012), 98.

Page 64: Dwight Moody, *Notes from My Bible: From Genesis to Revelation* (Chicago, IL: Fleming H. Revell, 1895), 8.

Page 66: Cited in Martin Manser, *The Westminster Collection of Christian Quotations* (Louisville, KY: Westminster John Knox Press, 2001), 363.

Page 68: Jen Wilkin, *Women of the Word: How to Study the Bible with Both Our Hearts and Our Minds* (Wheaton, IL: Crossway, 2014), 150.

Page 70: Nancy Leigh DeMoss, *A Place of Quiet Rest: Finding Intimacy with God Through a Daily Devotional Life* (Chicago, IL: Moody, 2000), 174.

Page 72: Cited in John Gillies, *Memoirs of Rev. George Whitefield* (Middletown, CT: Hunt & Noyes, 1838), 583.

Page 74: Charles Spurgeon, *The Complete Works of C. H. Spurgeon*, vol. 46: *Sermons 2603-2655* (Fort Collins, CO: Delmarva, 2013).

Page 76: Jerry Bridges, *The Practice of Godliness* (Colorado Springs, CO: NavPress, 2008), 32.

Page 78: Thomas Watson, *The Bible and the Closet: or How We May Read the Scriptures with the Most Spiritual Profit*, ed. John Overton Choules (Boston, MA: Gould, Kendall, & Lincoln, 1842), 25.

Page 80: J.I. Packer, *Knowing God* (Downers Grove, IL: InterVarsity Press, 1973), 23.

Page 82: John Piper, *Desiring God: Meditations of a Christian Hedonist* (Colorado Springs, CO: Multnomah Books, 2011), 154.

Page 84: Cited in Chelsea Patterson Sobolik, *Longing for Motherhood: Holding On to Hope in the Midst of Childlessness* (Chicago, IL: Moody, 2018).

Page 86: Cited in John Blanchard, *The Complete Gathered Gold* (Darlington, UK: Evangelical Press, 2006).

Page 88: J.C. Ryle, *Expository Thoughts on the Gospels : St. Matthew* (New York, NY: Robert Carter & Brothers, 1870), 172.

Page 90: Cited in David Jeremiah, *Discovering God: 365 Daily Devotions* (Carol Stream, IL: Tyndale House, 2015), 41.

Page 92: Merrill Unger, *The New Unger's Bible Handbook* (Chicago, IL: Moody, 2005), 13.

Page 94: Robert Chapman, *Choice Sayings: Being Notes of Expositions of Scripture* (London, ENG: Morgan and Scott, 1883), 7.

Page 96: Cited in Martin Manser, *The Westminster Collection of Christian Quotations* (Louisville, KY: Westminster John Knox Press, 2001), 19.

Page 98: Elisabeth Elliot, *On Asking God Why* (Ada, MI: Revell, 1989), 94.

Page 100: A.W. Tozer, *Of God and Men* (Harrisburg, PA: Christian Publications, 1960), 67.

Page 102: Jen Wilkin, *Women of the Word: How to Study the Bible with Both Our Hearts and Our Minds* (Wheaton, IL: Crossway, 2014), 31.

Page 106: E.M. Bounds, *The Complete Works of E.M. Bounds* (New York, NY: Start Publishing, 2012).

Page 108: Cited in "Quotes by Corrie ten Boom," GraceQuotes, https://gracequotes.org/author-quote/corrie-ten-boom/.

Page 110: D.A. Carson, *A Call to Spiritual Reformation* (Grand Rapids: Baker Academic, 1992), 208.

Page 112: Cited in "Quotes by E.M. Bounds," GraceQuotes, https://gracequotes.org/author-quote/e-m-bounds/.

Page 114: Cited in John Blanchard, *The Complete Gathered Gold* (Darlington, UK: Evangelical Press, 2006).

Page 116: H.B. Charles Jr., *It Happens After Prayer: Biblical Motivation for Believing Prayer* (Chicago, IL: Moody, 2013).

Page 118: H.B. Charles Jr., *It Happens After Prayer: Biblical Motivation for Believing Prayer* (Chicago, IL: Moody, 2013).

Page 120: Cited in David McCasland, *The Quotable Oswald Chambers* (Grand Rapids, MI: Oswald Chambers Publications Association, 2008).

Page 122: J.C. Ryle, *Expository Thoughts on the Gospels: St. John*, vol. 1 (New York, NY: Robert Carter & Brothers, 1874), 347.

Page 124: Hannah More, *Complete Works*, vol. 2 (New York, NY: Derby & Jackson, 1857), 515.

Page 126: Corrie ten Boom, *Clippings from My Notebook* (Nashville, TN: Thomas Nelson, 1982), 21.

Page 128: Cited in Alexander McConnell, William Revell Moody, and Arthur Percy Fitt, *Record of Christian Work* (East Northfield, MA: Record of Christian Work, 1920), 236.

Page 130: John Onwuchekwa, *Prayer: How Praying Together Shapes the Church* (Wheaton, IL: Crossway, 2018), 126.

Page 132: Paul Miller, *A Praying Life: Connecting with God in a Distracting World* (Colorado Springs, CO: NavPress, 2017).

Page 134: A.W. Pink, *Gleanings from Elisha, His Life and Miracles*, ed. Terry Kulakowski (Chicago, IL: Moody, 1981), 270.

Page 136: Timothy Keller, *Prayer: Experiencing Awe and Intimacy with God* (New York, NY: Penguin Books, 2016), 228.

Page 138: Cited in Terry Johnson, *When Grace Comes Alive: Living Through the Lord's Prayer* (Fearn, UK: Christian Focus Publications, 2003), 18.

Page 140: Thomas Watson, *A Divine Cordial—Romans 8:28* (Lafayette, IN: Sovereign Grace, 2001), 18.

Page 142: Megan Hill, *Praying Together: The Priority and Privilege of Prayer: In Our Homes, Communities, and Churches* (Wheaton, IL: Crossway, 2016), 39.

Page 144: Jeremy Taylor, *The Whole Works of the Right Rev. Jeremy Taylor D.D*, vol. 2 (London, England: Longman, Orme, Brown, Green, and Longmans, 1839), 145.

Page 146: R.A. Torrey, *The Power of Prayer and the Prayer of Power* (New York, NY: Cosimo, 2009), 136.

Page 148: Charles Spurgeon, *Spurgeon's Sermons*, vol. 7: *1861*, ed. Anthony Uyl (Woodstock, ON, 2017), 15.

Page 150: H.B. Charles Jr., *It Happens After Prayer: Biblical Motivation for Relieving Prayer* (Chicago, IL: Moody, 2013).

Page 152: J.C. Ryle, *Expository Thoughts on the Gospels: St. Matthew* (New York, NY: Robert Carter & Brothers, 1870), 182.

Page 154: Cited in John Blanchard, *The Complete Gathered Gold* (Darlington, UK: Evangelical Press, 2006).

Page 158: Michael Horton, in the foreword to Jonathan Leeman, *Church Membership: How the World Knows Who Represents Jesus* (Wheaton, IL: Crossway, 2012), 15.

Page 160: Jonathan Leeman, *Church Membership: How the World Knows Who Represents Jesus* (Wheaton, IL: Crossway, 2012), 32.

Page 162: Cited in "Quotes by Voddie Baucham," GraceQuotes, https://gracequotes.org/author-quote/voddie-baucham/.

Page 164: Michael Horton (@MichaelHorton_), Twitter, December 30, 2016, 2:38 a.m. https://twitter.com/MichaelHorton_.

Page 166: Kevin DeYoung, *The Hole in Our Holiness: Filling the Gap Between Gospel Passion and the Pursuit of Godliness* (Wheaton, IL: Crossway, 2012), 132.

Page 168: John Angell James, *Christian Progress: A Sequel to the Anxious Inquirer After Salvation* (New York, NY: American Tract Society, 1853), 119.

Page 170: John Blanchard, *The Complete Gathered Gold* (Darlington, UK: Evangelical Press, 2006).

Page 172: Charles Spurgeon, *The Metropolitan Tabernacle Pulpit*, vol. 41 (London, England: Passmore & Alabaster, 1895), 389.

Page 174: David Mathis, *Habits of Grace: Enjoying Jesus Through the Spiritual Disciplines* (Wheaton, IL: Crossway, 2016).

Page 176: Matthew Henry, *An Exposition of All the Books of the Old and New Testaments*, vol. 2 (London, England: W. Gracie, 1808), 70.

Page 178: Paul David Tripp, (@PaulTripp), Twitter, May 20, 2012, 7:59 a.m. https://twitter.com/PaulTripp.

Page 180: Philip Ryken, Derek Thomas, and Ligon Duncan, eds. *Give Praise to God: A Vision for Reforming Worship* (Phillipsburg, NJ: P&R Publishing, 2003), 65-68.

Page 182: Fred Craddock, *Preaching* (Nashville, TN: Abingdon Press, 2010).

Page 184: Cited in John Blanchard, *The Complete Gathered Gold* (Darlington, UK: Evangelical Press, 2006).

Page 186: Don Kistler, ed., *Feed My Sheep: A Passionate Plea for Preaching* (Orlando, FL: Soli Deo Gloria Ministries, 2002), 18.

Page 188: Cited in John Blanchard, *The Complete Gathered Gold* (Darlington, UK: Evangelical Press, 2006).

Page 190: R.T. Kendall, *Worshipping God: Devoting Our Lives to His Glory* (Lake Mary, FL: Charisma House, 2017).

Page 192: Leonard Ravenhill, *Why Revival Tarries* (Bloomington, MN: Bethany House, 2004).

Page 194: Bonnie Harvey, *D.L. Moody: Evangelizing the World* (Ulrichsville, OH: Barbour, 2006), 128.

Page 196: Matt Boswell, "Choosing Hymns," *Tabletalk* magazine, September 1, 2014.

Page 198: Keith and Kristyn Getty, *Sing!: How Worship Transforms Your Life, Family, and Church* (Nashville, TN: B&H, 2017).

Page 200: Mark Dever and Paul Alexander, *The Deliberate Church: Building Your Ministry on the Gospel* (Wheaton, IL: Crossway, 2005), 85.

Page 202: Jonathan Leeman, *Church Membership: How the World Knows Who Represents Jesus* (Wheaton, IL: Crossway, 2012), 90. Some of the content for this reading is drawn from New City Catechism, Question and Answer 44, available online at https://www.thegospelcoalition.org/new-city-catechism/what-is-baptism/.

Page 204: Bobby Jamieson, *Going Public* (Nashville, TN: B&H, 2015), 109.

Page 206: Mark Dever, "The Marks of the Church," *Tabletalk* magazine, March 1, 2008.

Page 210: William Secker, *The Nonsuch Professor in His Meridian Splendour; Or, the Singular Actions of Sanctified Christians, Laid Open in Seven Sermons* (Louisville, KY: Morton & Griswold, 1848), 117.

Page 212: "Quotes by Corrie ten Boom," GraceQuotes, https://gracequotes.org/author-quote/corrie-ten-boom/.

Page 214: Matthew Henry, *Matthew Henry's Commentary on the Whole Bible*, vols. 2-3, *Joshua to Second Samuel*, ed. Anthony Uyl (Woodstock, ON: Devoted Publishing, 2017), 459.

Page 216: Jerry Bridges, *Transforming Grace* (Colorado Springs, CO: NavPress, 1991), 127.

Page 218: Timothy Keller, *The Meaning of Marriage* (New York, NY: Dutton, 2011), 48.

ABOUT THE AUTHOR

Tim Challies is a Christian, a husband to Aileen, and a father to two girls in their teens and one son who is waiting for him in heaven. He worships and serves as an elder at Grace Fellowship Church in Toronto, Ontario. He is a blogger and book reviewer and has written a number of popular books. www.challies.com

ABOUT THE ILLUSTRATOR

Jules Koblun is an illustrator, designer, and art director living and working in the greater Toronto area. She is proficient in illustration, production design, digital content creation, marketing, typography, and project management. Jules has created SquareQuotes graphics for Tim Challies's blog since 2015. www.workbyjules.com